An Undivided Heart

*Pope John Paul II
on the
Deeper Realities
of the
Consecrated Life*

By Sr. Evelyn Ann Schumacher, O.S.F.

ISBN #0-9719524-0-x

ACKNOWLEDGMENTS

I wish to express my deep gratitude to His Eminence, Francis Cardinal George, O.M.I., Archbishop of Chicago, for writing the Preface.

I am greatly indebted to the Most Reverend Thomas G. Doran, President of the INSTITUTE ON RELIGIOUS LIFE, and to the entire Board of Directors for their willingness to publish *An Undivided Heart.*

Publically, I wish to thank the Knights of Columbus, especially the Supreme Knight Carl A. Anderson and his Board of Directors, who expressed their love for religious and priestly vocations and for our Holy Father's teaching by providing the necessary funds to produce, publish and promote this work.

Lastly, I owe special thanks to the following persons whose interest and valued suggestions, support and guidance made the completion and publication of this book possible: Rev. Thomas Nelson, O.Praem., Mr. Michael Wick, Mother Assumpta Long, O.P., and Mrs. Ann Carey.

Dedication

to the Franciscan Sisters of Christian Charity,
Manitowoc, Wisconsin

CONTENTS

PREFACE

In *Vita Consecrata*, the 1996 post-synodal apostolic exhortation of Pope John Paul II, the Holy Father opens with this statement: "The consecrated life, deeply rooted in the example and teaching of Christ the Lord, is a gift of God the Father to His Church through the Holy Spirit" (VC, 1). This one sentence encompasses all the deliberations and discussions of the bishops' gathering from around the world in Rome during the month of October, 1994. They reflected, prayerfully and practically, upon this wondrous gift from God, consecrated life in the Church.

Having been blessed to be one of the bishops present at this synod on consecrated life, I know how much the Holy Father esteems all forms of consecrated life and every man and woman who has taken religious vows. Pope John Paul II clearly recognizes the diversity of charisms which shape the many families of consecrated people, yet he insists that all of them exist to foster the personal holiness of their members and make visible the holiness of the Church.

The Church needs to reflect on the Holy Father's teachings in this important document and in his many addresses to those belonging to institutes of consecrated life. These texts contain the key for authentically unlocking the wealth contained in the documents of the Second Vatican Council. In learning from this study, those consecrated to the Lord with "an undivided heart" become signs of the "New Springtime" for the Gospel prayed for by the Pope. By their witness and ministry, they help transform the world into a civilization of love.

In her new book, Sr. Evelyn Ann Schumacher, O.S.F. has captured Pope John Paul's teaching on the consecrated life and its authentic renewal. She shows how consecrated life is necessary in the life of the Church and her members. She shows also how those who respond to the call to consecrated life are drawn into intimacy with both the Lord and His people. This is a much-needed book in this moment of the Church's life.

+ Francis Cardinal George, O.M.I.,
Archbishop of Chicago

FOREWORD

Reading the book, *An Undivided Heart,* by Sr. Evelyn Ann Schumacher, O.S.F., reminded me of the disciples' journey to Emmaus in which an unidentified traveler explained to them the meaning of Redemption, while their hearts burned with divine fervor. In Sister Evelyn Ann's book, the unidentified traveler is Christ in the person of his vicar, Pope John Paul II, who explains to religious the meaning of our life in the light of the mystery of the Redemption. One's heart burns with the fervor of divine love to give more as one hears Christ's vicar expound the meaning of the divine call to consecrate oneself totally to God in religious life.

Being a religious and former novice master of my community, I have always looked for good books and articles on religious life. Of all that I have read, I have found none better than the writings of John Paul II, who knows how to present the mystery of the consecrated life in such a compelling way as to draw one deeper into its mystery. The Holy Father speaks not as an academic theologian but as a successor of St. Peter and disciple of Jesus Christ who follows Him with "an undivided heart." He speaks from the abundance of his heart.

The Holy Father is well known for his teaching on marriage and family life. Many books have been written expounding his teaching, and institutes of higher learning have been founded to promote his thought on that vital and important subject. Of no less importance for the good of the Church in this new millennium, however, is his teaching on the mystery of the consecrated life. In a certain sense we can say that this teaching brings to fulfillment his instruction on marriage and family life, since religious life foreshadows the nuptial union of heaven to which marriage is ordered.

Pope John Paul II's writings on the subject of the consecrated life are voluminous and need to be presented in a way that renders them accessible to the Catholic laity and religious alike. This book hopes to answer that need.

As mentioned in the Introduction of this new work, the Holy Father's 1984 apostolic exhortation *Redemptionis Donum* addressed to women and men religious provides the seminal work to which all his reflections on religious life can be referred. The best commentary on *Redemptionis Donum* is found in the Holy Father's various addresses to consecrated persons. *An Undivided Heart* extends that commentary by weaving together John Paul II's exhortations to religious and other members of institutes of consecrated life, while focusing on his exhortation's central theme of the Redemption.

All the essential elements of religious life are treated in a way that not only instructs the mind, but also inspires the heart and elevates the soul to an undivided love for Christ. This book would therefore serve well as an introduction to the consecrated life for novices or those inquiring into it. It also will benefit those religious who have lived the vowed life for many years and are seeking personal renewal. Questions are provided for each chapter to stimulate further reflection and discussion.

The INSTITUTE ON RELIGIOUS LIFE is honored and happy to present this book on the teaching of John Paul II on the deeper realities of the consecrated life. I hope all who read it will find it helpful to better love and appreciate that mystery which is at the very heart of the Church and her Bridegroom, Jesus Christ.

—Rev. Thomas Nelson, O.Praem.,
IRL Executive Director

INTRODUCTION

From the very beginning of the Church, there were men and women who set out to follow Christ with greater liberty, and to imitate him more closely, by practicing the evangelical counsels. They led lives dedicated to God, each in his own way. Many of them, under the inspiration of the Holy Spirit, became hermits or founded religious families. These the Church, by virtue of her authority, gladly accepted and approved. Thus, in keeping with the divine purpose, a wonderful variety of religious communities came into existence.

—*Perfectae Caritatis, 1*

These reflections on the deeper realities of the consecrated life have been drawn mainly from the papal teachings presented in *John Paul II Speaks to Religious*, and *Redemptionis Donum*. In reminding religious of the priorities of their life of consecration, the Pope is shaping a theology of religious life that gives full coverage to those deeper realities that are sometimes unknown or overlooked. The purpose of this book is to encourage deeper reflection on the papal teachings on religious life which are presented in the above-mentioned sources.

John Paul II Speaks to Religious

A collection of the principal allocutions and letters of the Holy Father from 1978-1998 is found in a set of ten small volumes under the title, *John Paul II Speaks to Religious*. These teachings of the Pope have been compiled and arranged by Father Jean Beyer, S.J., Dean of the Faculty of Canon Law at the Gregorian University in Rome. The Little Sisters of the Poor are the distributors.

In his many special messages to religious, which are compiled in the Beyer volumes, the Holy Father reveals himself as a friend who loves and treasures religious communities. From the very beginning of his pontificate in 1978, the Pope has been deeply aware of the inestimable value of religious life to the Church. Throughout his pontificate he affirms forcefully that the consecrated life belongs in a distinct way to that spiritual fullness brought forth by the Holy Spirit for the good of the entire Church.

Furthermore, the Pope as a realist recognizes and faces the tremendous exterior and interior difficulties which assail the whole Church. With great clarity and enormous spiritual strength, Pope John Paul II has put forth every effort to exercise fully the unique duties of his office. Fully aware of his responsibility to God and the Church of our time, he has not only challenged religious to a generous witnessing to Christ in the midst of a highly secularized world, but he has also warned of the inherent dangers.

The numerous talks the Holy Father has given to religious around the world reveal profound knowledge of the Council in which he participated. He has at times spoken to individual congregations; at other times he has addressed large groups of many communities. While often calling attention to the special charisms of the specific founders and foundresses, the Holy Father's basic teachings on religious life are unambiguous explications of Vatican II teachings which apply to all men and women religious.

Redemptionis Donum

In 1984, at the close of the extraordinary Jubilee Year of the Redemption celebrating the 1,950th anniversary of the death and resurrection of Christ, Pope John Paul II gave to the Church an apostolic exhortation titled *Redemptionis Donum*. This writing is a word of love addressed to all men and women religious in which the Pope presents a new, profound and scripturally-based theology of religious consecration in light of the Mystery of the

Redemption.

However, does it not seem that this powerful and highly significant document has met with more or less indifference on the part of religious in general? History shows that some literary works do lie fallow for a while before they begin to exert their inner power. These writings become known as "seminal" writings. Might this writing of the Holy Father be a seminal work?

Clearly, this document gives full coverage to the deeper realities of the consecrated life. There in elegant and facile expression the Holy Father gives the profound spiritual meaning of the spousal relationship in all its beauty. Perhaps never before in the history of religious life have the vows of chastity, poverty and obedience been presented with such graceful force and spiritual profundity.

In this exhortation the Holy Father explains that Jesus Christ, who gives himself in the mystery of the Redemption, calls men and women to give themselves entirely to Him and to the work of the Redemption through membership in a community of brothers and sisters recognized and approved by the Church. He points out that since the special character of this particular Jubilee Year is precisely a call to conversion and reconciliation with God, we religious are urged to respond to this call by meditating more seriously on the manner in which we live our lives as consecrated persons in the light of the mystery of the Redemption. In this way, our lives will become fixed ever more firmly in that mystery.

While this call to conversion concerns everyone in the Church, it concerns men and women religious in a special way. Why? Because in our consecration to God through the evangelical counsels, we strive toward a particular fullness of the Christian life. Our special vocation and the whole of our life in the Church and the world take their character and spiritual power from following Christ along the "narrow and hard" way.

As noted above, it seems that *Redemptionis Donum* has received little recognition. However, due credit should be given to the Most Reverend John R. Sheets, S.J., who showed great interest in this document when it was published sixteen years ago.

While he was still teaching at Creighton University, Father Sheets gave retreats and wrote articles on *Redemptionis Donum*.

In writing this book I drew quite extensively from the audio tapes of a retreat he gave to a group of Carmelite Sisters in Danvers, Massachusetts. I also drew from his article, "The Primordial Mystery of Consecration" which appeared in the Sept./Oct. issue of *Review for Religious*, 1985.

Incidentally, I am indebted to Mr. Michael Wick, Director of Operations for the INSTITUTE ON RELIGIOUS LIFE, for the title of this book, *An Undivided Heart*. This phrase can be found in section 1 of *Vita Consecrata*: "In every age there have been men and women who, obedient to the Father's call and to the prompting of the Spirit, have chosen this special way of following Christ, in order to devote themselves to him with an 'undivided' heart" (cf. 1 Cor 7:34).

It is my hope that this mini-synthesis of the teachings of Pope John Paul II may serve to provide a glimpse into the practical theology of the consecrated life which is coming from the Pope himself.

CHAPTER 1

The Divine Call

The divine choice invites us to discover ourselves in the depths of the eternal mystery of God who is love.

—John Paul II, *Letter to All Consecrated Persons Belonging to Religious Communities and Secular Institutes,* May 22, 1988

A call from God can capture anyone, anywhere, at any time in life. It is a moment of singular and significant importance. Such a call is a personal summons from God Himself; its purpose is to accomplish the divine will. The explanation of the divine choice is love. No merit, no excellence can earn a call from God:

...the Lord set his love upon you and chose you.[1]

Accordingly, the person called becomes involved in an assignment directed by God Himself. Just as God awaited Mary's acceptance when Gabriel told her she would conceive and bear a son, so too, does He await the response of every person He calls.

Old Testament Calls

Among the most impressive pages of the Old Testament are those scenes which depict a personal call from God. There was the call of Abraham to leave Haran and go to the land of

Canaan. Abraham and his family had left Ur and settled in Haran, but Yahweh had other plans for him. He said:

> "Go from your country and your kindred and your father's house to the land that I will show you."[2]

Moses was called by God while he was tending the flock of his father-in-law, Jethro:

> "Come, I will send you to Pharaoh that you may bring forth my people, the sons of Israel, out of Egypt."[3]

Isaiah was called while he was praying in the temple. He heard the voice of Yahweh saying:

> "Whom shall I send, and who will go for us?"[4]

There was the dialogue between Yahweh and young Jeremiah:

> "Before I formed you in the womb I knew you, and before you were born I consecrated you; I appointed you a prophet to the nations."[5]

And there were many other calls. In every call we see God in His majesty and His mystery. To Moses he said:

> "Do not come near; put off your shoes from your feet, for the place on which you are standing is holy ground."[6]

Isaiah found himself in the heavenly court:

> "In the year that King Uzziah died, I saw the Lord sitting upon a throne, high and lifted up; and his train filled the temple."[7]

He heard the seraphim calling to one another:

> "Holy, holy, holy is the Lord of hosts; the whole earth is full of his glory." And the foundations of the threshold shook at the voice of the one who called and the house was filled with smoke.[8]

In every instance the human heart had the freedom to resist and the power to respond. In some instances, acceptance was freely given:

> So Abraham went as the Lord told him.[9]

And Isaiah responded with spontaneity and generosity:

"Here I am! Send me."[10]

But in other instances, fear gripped the heart of the one called. At first, Moses argued with Yahweh:

> "Oh my Lord, I am not eloquent ... but I am slow of speech and of tongue."[11]

Young Jeremiah was intimidated when the Word of the Lord came to him:

> "Ah, Lord God! Behold I do not know how to speak for I am only a youth."[12]

But Yahweh assured Jeremiah that all would be well:

> "Do not say, 'I am only a youth'; for to all to whom I send you, you shall go, and whatever I command you, you shall speak. Be not afraid of them for I am with you to deliver you."[13]

The Old Testament demonstrates that God always accompanies those who follow His call in faith and obedience.

New Testament Calls

The original members of the Church were chosen by Christ Himself. But before He called His first followers, Jesus spent the whole night in prayer. The next day He returned to the crowd and selected twelve men who were to be His constant companions. He selected these men without any thought of their talents or status in life. And He initiated them progressively into the secret of His mission and the mystery of His person.

What prompted Jesus to choose the twelve He called? He wanted to accomplish His mission by having with Him those He wished:

> And he went up into the hills, and called to him those whom he desired; and they came to him.[14]

The answer is found only in the mystery of God's choice.

Jesus demanded total detachment from His first followers. This meant the renunciation of riches and security, even the surrender of their respective families. And yet, the demand is still greater. Having renounced possessions and worldly attachments,

the disciples are told that they must follow the Master even to the
Cross:

> "If any man would come after me, let him deny himself
> and take up his cross and follow me."[15]

The Rich Young Man

In Chapter III of *Redemptionis Donum,* the Holy Father's apostolic exhortation to all men and women religious, the Pope
shares his reflections on the call to the consecrated life. He begins by centering on the gospel account of Jesus' dialogue with
the rich young man. He asks us to reflect on this encounter very
carefully because the dialogue that ensued during that brief meeting presents the interior structure and pattern of a call to a distinct kind of discipleship, namely, a call to follow Christ along the
path of the evangelical counsels.

Jesus is on the way to Jerusalem when a rich young man
runs up and kneels before Him. He has a question for Jesus:

> "Good Teacher, what must I do to inherit eternal life?"[16]

The Master proceeds to answer the question by reminding
him of the duties prescribed in the decalogue:

> "You know the commandments: 'Do not kill, Do not com-
> mit adultery, Do not steal, Do not bear false witness, Do
> not defraud, Honor your father and mother.'"[17]

Undismayed, the youth quickly informs Jesus:

> "All these I have observed; what do I still lack?"[18]

Even though he has always been a serious observer of the
law, this young man remains inwardly dissatisfied. He feels
called to do something more than just keeping the law. Attracted
to Jesus, the youth longs to become more closely associated
with Him. He has a sense of mystery, a longing for "the more"
found only in the deeper realities of human life. It is this desire
for "the more" that is rooted in the mysterious call to follow
Christ in the profession of the vows of poverty, chastity and
obedience.

The Eternal Son of the Father, invested with the Father's
love, stands there looking intently at this eager young man. The

Master begins by taking him "where he is," but now He offers him "the more:"

> And Jesus looking upon him loved him, and said to him, "You lack one thing; go, sell what you have, and give it to the poor, and you will have treasure in heaven; and come, follow me."[19]

The kind of discipleship to which Jesus is calling this would-be follower is costly. He is asked to sacrifice not only his social status, but the very root of his security. The man fails to measure up to this standard, not because he possesses great riches, but because they possess him. He lives not by faith but by holding on to what he has. Accordingly, he cannot move into spiritual freedom because he is controlled by earthly things.

Christ's admiration for this youth is obvious. Mark notes that Jesus looked at him and loved him. This is the love of the Redeemer, the love which reflects the eternal love of the Father who "so loved the world that he gave his only Son, that whoever believes in him should not perish but have eternal life."[20] Hence, the Father's love was revealed in the Son as redeeming love.[21]

Mark tells us that the young man went away sad. He reached up for "the more" and then fell back. His heart was heavy with the weight of refusal in his rejection of an offer to be a close associate of Jesus whom he so loved and admired.

From the beginning of His public life Jesus generally extended His call in the words: "Follow me." In making these appeals He shows the importance He attributed to Gospel discipleship for the life of the Church. Jesus links that discipleship with the "counsels" of consecrated life which He Himself lived and desired for His disciples.

In the Church today, vocations to religious life have no less importance than centuries past. The present vocation shortage in some parts of the world is a challenge to be met with determination, courage and prayer. We can be certain that Christ, who during His earthly life called many to the consecrated life, is still doing so in today's world.

CHAPTER 2

The Call to
Religious Profession

*First of all, the vocation which you received and which
was tested by your Congregation is a free gift of God's
love. Why you, rather than your sister or friend?*
—John Paul II to Women Religious in Lourdes, August 15, 1983

All Christians are called to follow Christ by living out the
maxims found in the Gospels. This is what is known as living the
evangelical life. Some Christians, however, are called to follow
Christ by living according to the greater demands of the Gospel
directives which call for a total commitment. This means leaving
everything behind:

> And everyone who has left houses or brothers or sisters
> or father or mother or children or lands, for my name's
> sake, will receive a hundredfold, and inherit eternal life.[1]

In other words, God does not require from everyone the
chastity, poverty and obedience to which we religious bind ourselves through our profession of the vows.

In his teachings on religious life the Holy Father explains that
many of the Gospel imperatives pertain only to what is necessary
for salvation, while the evangelical counsels take the Christian beyond that which is necessary. He reminds us that in the profession
of our vows, what we freely and generously give up are true values:
raising a family, owning personal property, and the full use of free

will. Yet, it is this precisely "going beyond" in our lives that draws us into a distinct sharing in Christ's own self-emptying and allows us to participate in a unique way in His own redemptive power.

The Divine Choice

In the call to the consecrated life all three divine Persons are involved. It is the Father who takes the initiative. He makes the choice. With divine intent He directs his "loving look" toward a particular person.

In *Vita Consecrata* we read that the event of the Transfiguration has special significance for those called to religious life. Just as the Father personally presented His Son to Peter, James and John on Mt. Tabor, so too does He present Him to the person of His choice:

> "This is my beloved Son, with whom I am well pleased; listen to him."[2]

Following this, the gentle force of the Father's deep and abiding love within draws the "chosen one," like a magnet, to His beloved Son:

> "No one can come to me, unless the Father who sent me draws him."[3]

The Son, who is the Way to the Father, now calls all those whom the Father has given to Him:

> "I am praying for them; I am not praying for the world but for those whom thou hast given me, for they are thine; all mine are thine, and thine are mine, and I am glorified in them."[4]

Just as Jesus looked with love on the rich young man, so now He fixes his loving gaze on the person given Him by the Father:

> "As the Father has loved me, so I have loved you; abide in my love."[5]

Accordingly, the call to religious profession has its ultimate source in the love with which the Father loves the Son. Those who let themselves be seized by this love cannot help but abandon everything to follow Him.[6]

This call can never be understood in human terms. So the Son now entrusts to the Holy Spirit the task of making it comprehensible to the human intellect and acceptable to the human heart. The one chosen by the Father begins to hear the call of Christ and with full trust in Him makes the decision to leave all in order to follow Him by living the life of the evangelical counsels. In *Vita Consecrata* we find a beautiful description of the role of the Holy Spirit in the discernment of a vocation to religious life:

> It is the Spirit who awakens the desire to respond fully; it is he who guides the growth of this desire, helping it to mature into a positive response and sustaining it as it is faithfully translated into action; it is he who shapes and molds the hearts of those who are called, configuring them to Christ, the chaste, poor and obedient one, and prompting them to make his mission their own. By allowing themselves to be guided by the Spirit on an endless journey of purification, they become, day after day, *conformed to Christ*, the prolongation in history of a special presence of the Risen Lord.[7]

In his 1984 apostolic exhortation to all men and women religious, the Holy Father views the call to religious profession in light of the mystery of the Redemption. He attributes this singular call to the redeeming love of Christ which reflects the Father's eternal love. He explains that the person called experiences an interior encounter with the redeeming love of Christ. The Holy Father writes:

> The call to the way of the evangelical counsels springs *from the interior encounter with the love of Christ*, which is a redeeming love. Christ calls precisely through this love of His. In the structure of a vocation, the encounter with this love becomes something specifically personal. When Christ "looked upon you and loved you," calling each one of you, dear religious, that redeeming love of His was directed towards a particular person, and at the same time it took on a *spousal character*; it became a *love of choice*. This love embraces the whole person, soul and body, whether man or woman, in that person's unique and unrepeatable personal "I."[8]

The Pope proceeds to explain that those who respond to this mysterious call to follow Christ are no longer their own, for they now belong to Christ because He bought them with a "price." Drawing from St. Paul's first letter to the Corinthians[9] the Holy Father writes:

> Yes, Christ's love has reached each one of you, dear brothers and sisters, with that same "price" of the Redemption. As a consequence of this, you have realized that *you are not your own but belong to Christ.* This new awareness was the fruit of Christ's "loving look" in the secret of your heart. You replied to that look by choosing Him who first chose each one of you, calling you with the measurelessness of His redeeming love. Since He calls "by name," His call always appeals to *human freedom.* Christ says, "If you wish...." And the response to this call, therefore, is a free choice. You have chosen Jesus of Nazareth, the Redeemer of the world, by choosing the way that He has shown you.[10]

In his many addresses to religious around the world, the Holy Father maintains that the evangelical counsels are not something that can be rationalized. He insists repeatedly that the profession of the vows of chastity, poverty and obedience is a response to a divine call, a love of choice. In other words, the evangelical counsels are not subject to human rationale, because they are rooted in the Gospel.

The Demands of Discipleship

In the Gospels the expression "follow me" always denotes attachment to the Person of Jesus. These words are a declaration of love coming from Jesus Himself. This is a call "which involves leaving everything behind (cf. Mt 19:27) in order to live at his side and to follow him wherever he goes (cf. Rev 14:4)."[11]

When Jesus called Simon and Andrew, his brother, and James and his brother John, they dropped what they were doing and went to Him immediately. There was something about Him that was irresistible. Once they became His disciples, they were initiated progressively into the mystery of His Person and the secret of His mission.

Having renounced possessions and worldly attachments, the disciple learns that he must follow Jesus even to the cross:

> Then Jesus told his disciples, "If anyone would come after me, let him deny himself and take up his cross and follow me."[12]

In demanding such a sacrifice from His followers, Jesus is not only requiring a sacrifice of one's possessions, but even of one's very person. However, the follower of Christ need not be apprehensive. Teresa of Jesus reminds us that "Christ is our model; whoever follows His counsels for the sake of pleasing Him has nothing to fear."[13]

Then, too, a disciple must follow Christ without any thought of following half-heartedly or of turning back. To the would-be follower, Jesus warned:

> "No one who puts his hand to the plow and looks back is fit for the kingdom of God."[14]

Here Jesus is telling His followers that the demand of the Kingdom is absolute. His call to follow Him signifies a life-long commitment. No other "need" may ever deter the disciple from following Him. Obviously, an ongoing response to the call to discipleship presupposes a special docility to the Holy Spirit. Without this inner disposition, authentic living and fidelity are not possible.

Religious Consecration: A Special Call

The vocation to the consecrated life is characterized by the call to be a disciple of Christ in a very special manner. In one of the general audiences on the consecrated life the Holy Father pointed out that "the purpose of religious life is to scale the heights of love: a complete love dedicated to Christ under the impulse of the Holy Spirit and, through Christ, offered to the Father...." The Pope maintains that this is the value of the oblation and consecration of religious profession.[15]

However, in order to walk in the footsteps of Christ, we religious must be prepared for trials and hardships. We can expect to share ever more consciously in the mystery of the passion, death and resurrection. In fact, we are meant to be a witness of the Paschal Mystery in a society corroded by the attraction of prosperity, eroticism and abuse of power. If we want to be faithful to our call, we have to put prayer at the center of our lives. This is essential if we want to live in close union with Christ in all the encounters and activities of our apostolates. Furthermore, we must maintain a vivid awareness of our vocation and live it in humility, always remembering that it is a gift from God. Lay people have need of witnessing this fidelity to our call.

This is the way that we religious surrender our lives to Jesus Christ in a free response to His "look of love." We do this by choosing to follow Him along the Gospel paths of chastity, poverty and obedience. The vows that we profess involve us personally on three basic levels: the level of feeling, of having and of power. If we live these counsels genuinely, they take on great meaning for us because each vow is meant to counteract the great unabating temptations that have assailed human nature since the time of Adam.

"To Be Perfect"

In section 4 of *Redemptionis Donum,* Pope John Paul II reflects again on Christ's words to the rich young man as they are recorded in the Gospel of Matthew:

> "If you would be perfect, go, sell what you possess and give to the poor, and you will have treasure in heaven; and come, follow me."[16]

For Matthew, perfection does not mean a higher form of morality to which only some Christians are called. On the contrary, all Christians are called to perfection. With his Old Testament background the evangelist sees "perfection" in terms of a direct and personal relationship with the living God Himself. He understands the word "perfect" to mean a whole-hearted dedication to doing God's will completely.

For this particular young man in the Gospel, God's will is clearly expressed. He is to sell his possessions and give the money to the poor. However, the ultimate demand of God's will which would make him perfect is not even love of neighbor. If he wishes to be perfect, he must follow Christ literally, all the way to Calvary. This means a willingness to accept the cross. Obviously, he cannot follow Christ with fidelity, if he does not love Him deeply.

Biblically, then, perfection is an interior attitude. It is found in the movement toward the person of Jesus Himself through the deliberate and daily surrender of one's total being to Him. The Pope's notion of perfection is biblical. In his apostolic exhortation to religious, he tells us that the call to perfection belongs to the very essence of the call to religious life. He explains that Christ's words, "Go, sell what you possess and give to the poor" unquestionably bring us into the realm of evangelical poverty. Clearly, these words are an invitation to us to let go of our attachment to those externals that feed our vanity and ego and thus to become more concerned about our inner life "with all the transcendence that is proper to it."[17]

To follow Christ radically means to move ever more closely to the person of Jesus through the daily abandonment of oneself to Him. It means to give ourselves to Him in a total and undivided way in our observance of poverty, chastity and obedience in the spirit of the Gospel. By our unique attachment to Christ we free ourselves from the self-destroying attachments to things, people and our own will. Thus, we religious begin to share in the "unfathomable richness of Christ" and become a true image of Him on earth.

Treasure in Heaven

Pope John Paul II is keenly aware of the tremendous difficulties that religious congregations face today. He searches out the roots of these difficulties and finds that the subtle and unspiritual pressures of a secular humanism are largely responsible.

In section 5 of *Redemptionis Donum* the Holy Father deals with the question, "How can one become more fully human?" He finds the answer in the gospel paradox of losing one's life in order to find it:

> "He who finds his life will lose it, and he who loses his life for my sake will find it."[18]

Basically this means that personal fulfillment sought for ego-centered purposes leaves one frustrated and empty; whereas, an ongoing "dying to self" in total surrender to the living person of Jesus Christ brings about an inner transformation which makes one more fully human. Here we have the basic law of death/resurrection which holds profound meaning for every serious "follower" of Christ. The Holy Father applies this to religious profession by returning to the episode of the rich young man.

Christ told this young man that if he would *go, sell* and *give*, he would have treasure in heaven. He explains that when a person sells what he possesses and gives to the poor, he begins to realize that those possessions and comforts he once enjoyed were not the things to hold on to. Such a person begins to discover a treasure within his own heart. And this treasure is indestructible because "it passes together with man into the dimension of the eternal."[19]

The Holy Father reminds us that Christ voluntarily gave up His body to redeem the world because He loved the world with infinite love. Religious, through the voluntary giving of their total being to Christ in their religious profession, immerse themselves in the Paschal Mystery of the redemption. This "step" in itself requires a renunciation which must be made in the spirit of sacrifice. And yet, it is not this step alone which brings about transformation in the heart of the religious. The Pope writes: "For a person discovers a new sense of his or her humanity, (the treasure within) not only in order to follow Christ but to the extent that he or she actually does follow Him."[20] Accordingly, we religious follow Christ and are gradually transformed by faithfully walking the demanding paths of the evangelical counsels. In this way we are given the "potential" to become just as He was: chaste, poor, obedient, humble, sacrificed, totally given to the Father's plan for the salvation of the human family.

In its most profound sense, the call to religious life is a call to spousal love. Full response to this call requires a return of love in a voluntary and ever-deepening abandonment of one's total being to Christ in all situations of life. The "treasure" then, is not so much a reward after death for good works achieved; rather, it is a rich and intimate relationship with the Person of the indwelling Christ even before death.

It is in this awareness of belonging to Jesus Himself that the heart, thoughts and deeds of the religious are transformed by His redemptive love. In short, it is in full response to the call to spousal love that a religious discovers the treasure within, enters into spiritual freedom and becomes more truly human. The religious thus witnesses to a world fragmented by illusion and strife the gospel paradox of losing one's life in order to find it.

CHAPTER 3

Religious Consecration:
A Sublime Mystery

Your vocation, dear brothers and sisters, has led you to religious profession, whereby you have been consecrated to God through the ministry of the Church, and have been at the same time incorporated into your religious family. Hence, the Church thinks of you, above all, as persons who are "consecrated": consecrated to God in Jesus Christ as His exclusive possession.

— John Paul II, *Redemptionis Donum, 7*

In recent years the word "consecration" in connection with religious life has taken on somewhat ambiguous and negative overtones. The reason for this attitude seems to be a failure to grasp the full and true meaning of consecration. In losing sight of consecration in this sense, we tend to lose sight of the fundamental reality of religious life. As a matter of fact, a view of religious life stripped of this essential element would necessarily be a non-Christian view.

In an article, "The Primordial Mystery of Consecration," John Sheets, S.J. (later Bishop Sheets), stresses the need to recapture the primordial meaning of consecration. He explains that consecration is not something that touches us merely externally; nor does it connote being apart or separated from the world.

Rather, it is the overflow of the sacred into our world. Thus, the mystery of consecration has something to do with the sacred or divine entering the human realm; that which is out of time and space becomes concretized in time and space. In other words, that which belongs to God alone, His own divine *milieu*, so to speak, becomes our *milieu*. This is sheer gift from God Himself.[1]

The Mission of the Son

The Church is more than a mere human agency or a "do-good" organization. Even though it is a reality in the temporal order, it is imbued with the hidden presence of God. The mission of the Church in the world is a continuation of Christ's own mission assigned to Him by the Father. By nature this mission is redemptive because its purpose is the transformation of the world and the salvation of all people.

Every mission involves at least two persons: the sender and the one sent. The one sent is to accomplish the purpose designated by the sender. At a specific time in human history, the Father who loves the world with incredible love sent His Son to earth in order to bring back to Him the work of creation which had been contaminated by sin. In his apostolic exhortation to religious, the Pope reminds us that man especially "must be given and restored to God, if he is to be fully restored to himself."[2]

The Son "consecrated" Himself by putting Himself wholly at the disposal of the Father so that by His obedience He might bring about our redemption.[3] In her meditations on the farewell discourses in the Gospel of John, Adrienne Von Speyr speaks of that kind of obedience which brought about the redemption of the world. She writes:

> Obedience is the most divine and most human expression and proof of love. Love wants to obey; it wants only to do the will of the beloved and does not even want to be considered while doing so. Not because of "self-denial," "self-sanctification," "mortification" or any other ascetic training, but out of the simplest necessity of love itself. In all weakness, yet totally resolved, it offers itself: "Do with me as you will."[4]

Through His death and resurrection the Son accomplished His mission in an extremely narrow and limited circle and then He returned to His Father. It was the Father's will, however, that the mission be extended to the whole world. With Christ no longer present in His human form, how could this be done?

When the risen Lord appeared to the disciples that first Easter evening, they were filled with joy at sight of Him. After wishing them peace and showing them His hands and side, He said, "As the Father sent me, so I am sending you."[5]

At this time, Jesus is asking His followers to undertake, in their turn, the very mission He undertook for the Father and to work in His name as He worked in the name of the Father. As the Father sent the Son, so the Son sends His own in obedience. He entrusts to them the whole of His mission.

It is obvious, however, that the disciples could not carry on the divine mission with their own human powers alone. That is why the Holy Spirit was sent. The Spirit of truth was sent to proclaim the revelation of the Son and to empower, guide and make holy. This Spirit would be passed on to other believers in the sacrament of Baptism.

In his teachings on the consecrated life the Holy Father roots religious life in the redemptive mission of Jesus Christ. When Christ called us to follow Him along the narrow way of the evangelical counsels, He bestowed upon each of us a look of redeeming love which embraced our whole being. Our ongoing and ever-deepening response to this "look of love" requires a close following of Him who was "missioned" by the Father. Consequently, all those who bind themselves to the chaste, poor and obedient Christ by publicly vowing to live radical chastity, poverty and obedience, have no choice but to share in His mission of redeeming the human family.

In his many addresses to religious around the world, the Holy Father repeatedly encourages us to follow Christ radically. He tells us that love for the person of Christ and dedication to His redemptive work is the basic option of our life. Thus, consecrated and bound to Christ we become the means through which the salvific action of God Himself flows out into the lives of others.

The Consecrated One — *Par Excellence*

Ordinarily, the consecrated life is perceived as a human insti-
tution that comes from the initiative of Christians who wanted to
live the Gospel ideals more deeply. But in a general audience on
October 12, 1994, the Holy Father clearly stated that Christ Himself is the founder of religious life. While it is true that He did not
directly found any religious community as such, yet, He did establish the state of the consecrated life in its overall values and essential elements. From Gospel testimony we learn that Christ was
consecrated by the Father. We learn, too, that He instituted and
was the first to live out the evangelical counsels. In this sense,
He is the founder of religious life.[6]

In an address to an international congress of religious in 1992,
the Holy Father stressed the need for a return to Gospel sources.
He then told this group that we should look to Jesus Christ as the
unparalleled example of a consecrated person who "sent into the
world, calls his disciples to follow him through the radical gift of
self to the heavenly Father and to the faithful."[7]

The Pope then turned to the Gospel of Luke to show that the
Holy Spirit is the principle of the "consecration" and "mission" of
the Messiah:

> And he came to Nazareth where he had been brought
> up; and he went to the synagogue, as his custom was on
> the sabbath day, and he stood up to read; and there was
> given to him the book of the prophet Isaiah. He opened
> the book and found the place where it was written, "The
> Spirit of the Lord is upon me, because he has anointed
> me to preach good news to the poor ...."[8]

When He finished the reading, Jesus closed the book, gave it
back to the attendant and sat down. All eyes in the synagogue
were fixed on Him. He then told His fellow townsmen, "Today
this scripture has been fulfilled in your hearing."[9]

So it is in the synagogue of Nazareth that Jesus applies
Isaiah's messianic prophecy to Himself. And He fully understands His own mission in fulfilling the ancient prophecy. It follows then, that this young man from Nazareth is the "Consecrated One" – *par excellence*. He is God's Anointed, the "Christ."
This means that "The Spirit of the Lord" penetrates every part of

His being, reaching to the very depths of all that He is and does. Indeed, it is this unique presence of the Holy Spirit within Him who unites His mission with His consecration in an unbreakable bond.[10]

In light of the consecration of Jesus whom "God anointed ... with the Holy Spirit and with power" (Acts 10:38), we perceive the Father, the fount of all holiness, as the ultimate source of the consecrated life. Jesus is the one "whom the Father consecrated and sent into the world" (Jn 10:36). Accepting His consecration by the Father, the Son in turn consecrates Himself to the Father for the sake of humanity:

> "And for their sake I consecrate myself that they also may be consecrated in truth."[11]

Christ's own life of virginity, obedience and poverty clearly demonstrates His complete filial acceptance of the Father's plan for the redemption of the world. His will was always in total compliance with the will of the Father:[12]

> "For I have come down from heaven, not to do my own will but the will of Him who sent me."[13]

With full trust in Christ, we religious can look to Him as our sublime model of the consecrated life. He has called us to follow Him by doing not our own will but the will of the Father through our own unreserved gift of self to Him "for the sake of humanity."[14]

Religious Consecration

In Chapter III of *Redemptionis Donum* the Holy Father reminds us that our first consecration occurs when we are baptized. Indeed, it is the sacrament of Baptism which draws us into the Paschal Mystery, the apex and center of the redemption accomplished in Christ. This means that in this sacrament the Christian is taken into the *milieu* of Christ's own death and resurrection. Here, the Self-gift of God in the Person of the Holy Spirit gives the Christian an entirely new identity, an identity which makes possible the transformation of the whole person. Here in this sacred *milieu* the inner person is transformed and redemption takes place.

The Holy Father then proceeds to reinforce the teachings of *Perfectae Caritatis* by reminding us that while deeply rooted in baptismal consecration "religious profession is a fuller expression of it." He explains that it is a new burial in the death of Christ: new, because it is made with awareness and by choice; new, because of love and vocation; new, by reason of increasing conversion.[15]

Thus, religious profession creates a new bond between the religious and the triune God in Jesus Christ. It is new and special in the way that it bears witness to the two different but inseparable aspects of the Paschal Mystery, namely, the death and resurrection of Jesus Christ. While both the baptismal consecration and the religious profession have their ultimate foundation in Christ crucified, yet, the profession of the evangelical counsels constitutes a new life "for God in Jesus Christ." Since religious profession consists in making a voluntary sacrificial and total gift of self to God in a much more mature and conscious manner, the "old nature is put off" and likewise "the new nature is put on." The uniqueness of religious consecration, then, is in the distinct way it renders visible and efficacious the "paschal duality" that lies at the very heart of the Church.[16]

In other words, our commitment as religious results from a choice made first by Christ Himself. And in our profession of the evangelical counsels we offer our lives as a free response to this choice; we freely and publicly "lay down our lives," as it were. Such a step amazes the world. Truly, this commitment would be nothing but folly were it not made in friendship with the Lord.

A Covenant of Spousal Love

Isaiah had astonishing news for the whole of humanity when he announced that the transcendent Creator, the Lord of the universe, claims each and every person as His very own possession:

> "Fear not, for I have redeemed you; I have called you by name, you are mine."[17]

Just as God once spoke through the prophet Isaiah, so does He speak to each of us. In addressing a large group of priests and religious in 1990, the Holy Father spoke of the covenant made between the Lord and His people. He called their attention to the fact that the prophets of the Old Testament placed the relationship between God and humanity within the context of marital love. "Every man, every woman is the object of God's special love and it is a marital love," the Pope said.[18]

In the New Testament, Baptism allows God's love to expand in our hearts through the Holy Spirit. The Pope explains that religious life placed in the context of a continuation of Baptism, "displays within the Church this wonderful spousal union which God wants to establish within us and which is the sign of the age to come."[19]

In Chapter III of *Redemptionis Donum,* the Holy Father uses the above quote from Isaiah in his introduction to the section on "A Covenant of Spousal Love." He explains that the Lord speaks to each religious as He once did to the prophet Isaiah. He points out that Christ's call, "If you would be perfect ... follow me," is prompted by His redeeming love. Simply put, this means: "Don't be afraid because I have bought you back. I have called you by name and you are a special possession of mine." Anything "bought back" is bought back because it is really wanted. Sometimes at a huge price. It then becomes a special possession of the owner.

Furthermore, being called by name means that God knows us in our depths as no one else knows us. In fact, there is no aspect of our being that is unexplored by the Spirit. And to us Christ says, "You are mine!" This is what the Holy Father means when he says that the call to follow Christ according to the evangelical counsels comes from the depths of the redemption and from that depth it reaches the human heart. [20]

Our answer to this call is also an answer of love, an answer in the gift of self to God. It is this voluntary gift of one's total being to Christ Himself that draws us into the mystery of *spousal union*. In other words, my call to religious life is a profound expression of the love of God for me. And my free and full response to this "love of choice" creates a special relationship between Christ and myself. This means that I give my total and undivided devotion to no other person than Christ Himself.

In his teachings on religious life, the Holy Father attempts again and again to raise our consciousness not to something new but to something that has always been there: our special sharing as religious in the Redeemer's death on the cross and His rising to new life. The practice of total self-giving in living the spirit of the counsels inevitably involves the cross as the condition for following Christ closely. Only in this way is rebirth to new life made possible.

The Pope then proceeds to remind us that our words of self-offering are actually an echo of Christ's own words, Who, when He came into the world said to the Father:

> "You have prepared a body for me ... lo, I have come to do your will."[21]

In this self-offering of Christ to His Father, we find both spousal and redemptive love. For love He offered Himself and for love He gave His body "for the sins of the world."

The Holy Father urges us religious to immerse ourselves in the Paschal Mystery of the Redeemer by offering our bodies as a sacrifice. In this way the likeness of that love which in the heart of Christ is both redemptive and spousal, is imprinted on the religious profession. Our love for Christ becomes spousal and our love for others becomes redemptive. Furthermore, interior freedom and genuine spiritual maturity are the gifts granted to those who "lose their life" for the sake of Christ. The Holy Father then explains that this is the beginning of our new life in Christ and in the Church. At the same time it is the beginning of "the new creation."[22]

In his many addresses to consecrated men and women religious, the Holy Father regularly reminds us that the radical nature of our self-giving sustained by constant dialogue with the Lord deters us from yielding to "the spirit of the times." He repeatedly tells us that our intimate and profound knowledge of Christ is actuated and deepened from day to day through faithfulness to personal, communal and liturgical prayer. He claims that this is the only way of moving into intimacy with our heavenly Bridegroom.

Consequently, called to deep intimacy with our divine Spouse by our profession of the evangelical counsels, we religious proclaim that Christ is to be loved by an undivided heart (chastity), embraced as our priceless treasure (poverty) and obeyed as our only Lord (obedience). We should love Him in a way that befits our spousal state: by adopting His sentiments, by sharing His manner of life, a life of humility and gentleness, of love and mercy, of service and joyful availability and of untiring zeal for the Father's glory and the salvation of the human race.[23]

Thus, it can be said that it is this divine and human mutual self-giving that is at the heart of religious consecration, for it is in the mystery of spousal union that I belong to God in an exclusive way. It follows, then, that in this "belonging" I become Christ's possession and He becomes mine.

CHAPTER 4

The Evangelical Counsels:
A Radical Following of Christ

The internal purpose of the evangelical counsels leads to the discovery of yet other aspects that emphasize the close connection of the counsels with the economy of the Redemption. We know that the economy of the Redemption finds its culminating point in the Paschal Mystery of Jesus Christ, in whom there are joined self-emptying through death and birth to new life through resurrection.

–Pope John Paul II, *Redemptionis Donum*, 10

The word "redemption" is a term used to describe a deep mystery. It is a favorite term in Scripture and, obviously, a favorite term in the Holy Father's own spirituality.

Redemption is a gift. Like any other gift, it demands the free response of acceptance or rejection. The gift of redemption originates in the love of the Father who sent His Son to redeem the world. It is His unquenchable desire to give Himself in total love that moved the Father to send the Son. Since the Father's self-gift in the Son is prompted by total love, the gift of redemption is spousal. And since spousal love is always sacrificial, it is likewise redemptive. When we respond by allowing ourselves to be redeemed by God's love, through the abandonment of our total self to Him, we open ourselves to ever deeper union with Him.

In his treatment of the economy of the redemption in Chapter IV of *Redemptionis Donum*, the Holy Father shares his insights regarding a definite correlation between the profession of the evangelical counsels and this "economy."

The Economy of Redemption

The word "economy" is sometimes applied to the way a household is run. It implies a plan and careful administration. When applied to the redemption, "economy" simply means God's overall plan and activity in the unfolding of human history. It means that God's plan for "running His household" is to call all people to enter into a personal relationship with Him.

In section 9 of his apostolic exhortation to men and women religious, the Holy Father reminds us once again that the full gospel message contains many exhortations or counsels. Some of these pertain only to what is necessary for salvation; however, the evangelical counsels take the Christian beyond that which is necessary. He states that "chastity, poverty and obedience give to that way a particular *Christocentric characteristic*, and imprint upon it a specific sign of the economy of the Redemption."[1] In a word, it is precisely this "going beyond" that gives the practice of the counsels a Christocentric characteristic.

It follows, then, that this distinct "characteristic" creates in the heart of the religious a special bond of communion with Christ, and in Him, with the Holy Trinity. Consequently, this distinguishing "attribute" which is imprinted on the religious consecration gives the religious a special role in the economy of the redemption. In 1985 the Holy Father addressed a group of religious in Quito, Ecuador. He told them: "Your consecrated life allows you to enter into the Heart of God in order to harmonize with his designs for the salvation of all."[2]

Redemptive Love

In the first letter of John, the word "world" is used in two different ways: at times it refers to the good world as it comes from God, and at other times it refers to a world that is evil and resistant to God. In section 9 of *Redemptionis Donum,* the Holy Father quotes a passage from 1 John in which he reflects on the implication of the second meaning. The passage reads:

> Do not love the world or the things of the world. If anyone loves the world, love for the Father is not in him. For all that is in the world, the lust of the flesh, and the lust of the eyes and the pride of life, is not of the Father but is of the world. And the world passes away, and the lust of it; but he who does the will of God abides forever.[3]

In this passage John mentions three sins that are typical of the "passing world": the lust of the flesh, the lust of the eyes and the pride of life. The Pope explains that none of these characteristics could ever come from the Father. On the other hand, they are "hidden within man as the inheritance of original sin, as a result of which the relationship of the world, created by God and given to men to be ruled by him, was disfigured in the human heart in various ways."[4]

The word "world" as used in the above quote means human society in so far as it operates on principles which are contrary to God's principles. This world is characterized by illusions that spring out of subtle and non-spiritual pressures coming from a secular humanism. In this "world," standards tend to be merely those commonly accepted by the society in which one lives. Even though mores and lifestyles dictated by "the ways of the world" may be socially acceptable, they are not necessarily compatible with the ways of God.

In his letter to religious, the Holy Father then proceeds to explain how the threefold lust is conquered. He writes:

> Religious profession places in the heart of each one of you, dear brothers and sisters, the love of the Father: that love which is in the heart of Jesus Christ, the Redeemer of the world. It is love which embraces the whole world and everything in it *that comes from the Father,* and which at the same time tends to overcome in the world everything that "does not come from the Father." It tends, therefore, to conquer the threefold lust.[5]

Christ speaks of His love for the world in the context of His redemptive work, that is, the laying down of His life for His friends.

The Holy Father frequently reminds us that we are to love others as Christ has loved us. This means that we must see our religious consecration as a "laying down" of our lives for the salvation of others.

Paschal Dimension of the Consecrated Life

As Catholics, we believe that the redemption of the world is rooted in the Paschal Mystery of Jesus Christ, in whom we find both self-emptying through death, and birth to new life through resurrection. Clearly, the evangelical counsels have a profound paschal dimension since they presuppose an identification with Christ in His death and resurrection.

In 1984, the Holy Father spoke to a group of men and women religious in Seoul. He said that together with all the baptized, but in a fuller way by reason of their religious consecration, they share in our Savior's cross. He explained that religious life, like martyrdom, is a special invitation by God to become the "grain of wheat that dies." He then assured them that this "dying in Christ" brings forth abundant fruit and leads to eternal life.[6]

In section 10 of *Redemptionis Donum* the Holy Father maintains that as we religious live out the evangelical counsels in ever greater refinement, the more deeply are we drawn into the Paschal Mystery of Jesus Christ. In this way the "roots" of sin within us (death) are gradually destroyed, and the more profound good hidden in each of us is brought forth (resurrection). The Holy Father calls this ongoing death-resurrection experience "paschal duality." He writes:

> The practice of the evangelical counsels contains a deep reflection of this paschal duality, the inevitable destruction of what in each of us is sin and its inheritance, and the possibility of being reborn each day to a more profound good hidden in the human soul.[7]

What does the Holy Father mean when he speaks of a more profound good hidden in each soul? And how is this "good" awakened? He points out that it is through the practice of the counsels that the human heart is "sensitized," and the good that may be lying dormant comes to life, as it were. This takes place, of course, through the mysterious action of the Holy Spirit:

The entire economy of the Redemption is realized precisely through this sensitivity to the mysterious action of the Holy Spirit, the direct Author of all holiness.[8]

Furthermore, this profound "good" becomes manifest in a unique awareness of one's own deep needs and the deep needs of others, along with a clear understanding of the will of the Father in meeting these needs.

In light of the above, it is obvious that the distinguishing feature about the vows is their paschal character. That is their very nature! Is not the paschal character of chastity, poverty and obedience, then, the only criterion that can be applied to the counsels? Is it not the only norm that can tell us how they should be lived? Is it not the only way that religious can become truly free in order to serve others in a truly Christ-like way? Can anyone, then, at any period in history, really change the very nature of the evangelical counsels by anchoring them in the subtle attractions of secular humanism?

No, the "paschal duality" which constitutes the very nature of the vows will always remain unchanged, for these counsels are rooted in the Gospel paradox of:

"giving up" in order "to give to,"

"self-emptying" in order "to fill,"

"letting go" in order "to open oneself to the always more."

And to what purpose? As consecrated persons share more and more deeply in the "self-emptying of Christ" we share more immediately and profoundly in that love which the Father and the Son have for each other in the Holy Spirit. Thus, we become empowered to reflect the splendor of this love which brings forth bountiful redemptive fruit not only in each one's own life, but also in the lives of others.[9]

Redemption of the World

In his addresses to religious, the Holy Father often reminds us that the apostolic nature of the consecrated life is to shape the world. It is to activate the redemptive love of Christ in order to bring about a new creation. Thus, in a most paradoxical way the self-limitations of chastity, poverty and obedience become most creative.

St. Paul seems to be a favorite of Pope John Paul II. In section 9 of *Redemptionis Donum,* he cites this great apostle who sensed so well that the whole world would be transformed through God's wonderful economy of the redemption:

> For the creation waits with eager longing for the revealing of the sons of God ... and will be set free from its bondage to decay and obtain the glorious liberty of the children of God.[10]

The Holy Father then proceeds to explain that the transformation of the world will take place when redemption finds its abode in the human heart. Through the authentic living of chastity, poverty and obedience, the heart of the religious is transformed and such religious help to overcome in the world everything that "does not come from the Father." When mankind finds deliverance from bondage and enters into the glorious liberty of the children of God, nature will experience in her own way a parallel freedom from all disordered activity.

In the economy of the redemption, then, the evangelical counsels constitute the most radical means for transforming the "world" because they are the most radical means for transforming the human heart. The Pope writes:

> *Evangelical chastity* helps us to transform in our interior life everything that has its source in the lust of the flesh; *evangelical poverty*, everything that finds its source in the lust of the eyes; and *evangelical obedience* enables us to transform in a radical way that which in the human heart arises from the pride of life .... *The evangelical counsels* in their essential purpose aim at "the renewal of creation": "the world," thanks to them, is to be subjected to man and given to him in such a way that man himself may be perfectly given to God.[11]

Thus, living out the true meaning of the evangelical counsels takes the religious beyond what is necessary for salvation. Indeed, the profession of the vows of chastity, poverty and obedience binds those of us who are religious to renounce not only what is sinful, but even many things that are legitimate. It is this "going beyond" that gives the practice of the counsels a unique participation in Christ's own self-emptying and rising to new life. In a word, it is in our indissoluable union with Him in His personal death and resurrection that we share in a unique way in His own redemptive power.

Clearly, then, our vocation consists precisely in entering into this mysterious union with Christ by dying daily to self and rising to new life in union with Him who is the Redeemer of the world. Accordingly, it is in this union that we live out our role in the economy of the redemption and thus become His "collaborators" in the redemption of the world. What could be more fulfilling?

CHAPTER 5

Consecrated Chastity

The chastity of celibates and virgins, as a manifestation of dedication to God with an undivided heart (cf. 1 Cor 7:32-34), is a reflection of the infinite love which links the three divine Persons in the mysterious depths of the life of the Trinity, the love to which the Incarnate Word bears witness even to the point of giving his life, the love "poured into our hearts through the Holy Spirit" (Rom 5:5), which evokes a response of total love for God and the brethren.

–John Paul II, *Vita Consecrata,* 21

The evangelical counsels are a gift from the Trinity. They are an expression of the love of the Son for the Father in the unity of the Holy Spirit. Accordingly, if we want to comprehend the counsels in their most profound meaning, we must view them in relation to the Trinity. The complete intimacy and communion of life present in the Trinity are revealed in these wondrous words found in the prologue of St. John's Gospel:

> No one has ever seen God; the only Son, who is in the bosom of the Father, he has made him known.[1]

In St. John's account of the Last Supper, we find the beloved disciple leaning on the breast of Christ. Symbolically, John represents the Church. The Church is in the bosom of Christ and Christ is in the bosom of His Father. Is it any wonder that Christ called Himself the Bridegroom of the Church?

The counsel of chastity is addressed in a distinct way to the love of the human heart. This love is a gift presented to us by God Himself. It is "poured" into our hearts by the Holy Spirit in the sacrament of Baptism. In living the life of the counsels, the consecrated person lives with special intensity the love of the Son for the Father through the action of the Holy Spirit.

Consecrated chastity, however, places greater emphasis on the spousal character of this love, while poverty, and still more obedience, emphasize primarily the aspect of redemptive love. Since the consecrated life is rooted in "spousal love," chastity is the foundation for poverty and obedience, for without chastity, the other two would have no meaning.[2]

Nuptial Imagery in the Old Testament

In the Old Testament we read about Yahweh's promise to espouse Himself to a people through the making of a covenant. The prophets in particular used the marriage imagery freely to describe the relationship between Yahweh and the chosen people. Hosea, for instance, employed spousal language in his portrayal of the unique bonding between God and the Israelites. This symbolic marriage "contract" expresses the depth and intimacy of God's love for the people of Israel:

> "And I will betroth you to me forever; I will betroth you to me in righteousness and in justice, in steadfast love and in mercy. I will betroth you to me in faithfulness, and you shall know the Lord."[3]

In the Hebrew language the words, "I will betroth you" signify the bridal gift the husband bestowed on the bride. If we take these words literally, they mean that God will share with His people His own attributes of integrity, justice, tenderness and love. What an astonishing act of divine "self-gift" this is! Just as God's plans are unchangeable, so is this marriage bond unchangeable.

Since a marriage contract always involves mutual self-giving, this divine gift of Self on the part of Yahweh called for a corresponding "gift of self" on the part of the chosen people. Through loving trust, deep affection and joyful submission to the divine will, the Israelites would come to "know" Yahweh. This knowledge, however, would be more than merely intellectual. Through the acceptance of His love and the giving of their own love to Him, it would mean an experience of the reality of Yahweh and His divinity. To know fully would mean the perfection of knowledge merging into the perfection of love.[4]

Virginity: A New Mode of Love

Such nuptial imagery has a tradition not only in the Old Testament, but in the New Testament as well. While the covenant bonding in the Old Testament was unique, it did not bring forth the true meaning of virginity. For the Jew, love, life, marriage and a large family were a sign of God's blessing. Not to be married and not to have a family were viewed as a curse.

With the Incarnation, however, the reality behind "spousal imagery" deepens, and a whole new mode of love emerges. This reality is a profound mystery, the mystery of the new relationship hinted at in Hosea when he speaks of Yahweh's betrothal to His people.

Accordingly, it is only when God takes on human flesh and gives Himself to us by giving Himself for us that this new mode of love finds expression. In the action of Christ, "This is My Body given for you" and "This is My Blood poured out for you," we have a unique and most mysterious bonding of God with His people. The reality here is that what is given for us brings about union and oneness with Christ Himself. In this sacrificial offering of Himself, Christ washes us clean, puts a wedding garment on us, as it were, and takes us to Himself.

However, this new mode of love which brings about union with God became available to believers only through the coming of the Holy Spirit on Pentecost. Within this tiny group of believers there gradually emerged a sense of the mystery of this love, a sense of the mystery of virginity, of chastity.

Very early in the history of the Church, St. Paul had insight into this mystery when he began to see virginity as the single-hearted devotion to Christ by an individual person. He resorted to daring imagery when he perceived virginity as a mode of love analogous to that of husband and wife. It is within this context that we have the origin of this single-minded dedicated love of Christ which we call consecrated chastity. By the end of the first century, there was a growing tendency in the Church to regard abstinence from marriage as a sign of holiness.[5]

"For the Sake of the Kingdom of Heaven"

In professing the counsel of chastity, the consecrated person renounces the temporal joys of married and family life. In *Redemptionis Donum* the Pope quotes the words of Christ Himself who used an image that referred to a well-known fact, the condition of a eunuch:

> "There are eunuchs who have made themselves eunuchs for the sake of the kingdom of heaven. He who is able to receive this, let him receive it."[6]

The Holy Father then comments on the last line of this quote. He notes that these words are a clear indication that this invitation is a counsel; it is not meant for everyone. He sees it as an expression of spousal love for the Redeemer Himself.

The Pope then proceeds to explain further the meaning of Christ's words "to make themselves eunuchs for the sake of the kingdom of heaven." This does not mean merely giving up marriage and family life. It also has a positive aspect in the charismatic choice of Christ as one's exclusive Spouse. This "special mode of love" which moves one to choose Christ is a gift which can come only from God Himself. "He who is able to receive it, let him receive it," Jesus says.[7]

The Holy Father then draws from Paul's first letter to the Corinthians. The apostle states that they "do well" who choose matrimony but they "do better" who choose virginity. However, lest he be misunderstood, the Pope hastens to explain that we do not find in the words of Christ or of Paul any depreciation of marriage or lack of esteem for matrimony. Actually, true married love is caught up in God's love, and Christ Himself who is the Bridegroom of the Church meets Christian husbands and wives in the sacrament of Matrimony.[8]

To show that those who choose virginity should be free from the anxieties of married life, the Pope quotes directly from Paul's letter:

> The unmarried man is anxious about the affairs of the Lord, how to please the Lord ... and the unmarried woman or girl is anxious about the affairs of the Lord, how to be holy in body and spirit.[9]

Obviously, the choice of Christ as one's exclusive Spouse certainly enables the consecrated person to be "anxious about the affairs of the Lord." However, since this choice is made "for the sake of the kingdom of heaven," it also empowers one to bring the eschatological kingdom of God close to the lives of people in the here and now. In other words, this "special mode of love" which is chastity renders present and makes real a reality that cannot be seen. What does this mean?

Through the vow of chastity, consecrated persons "having made themselves eunuchs for the sake of the kingdom of heaven" announce the future resurrection and eternal life, namely, life in union with God Himself. They are symbols and witnesses that anticipate heavenly life here on earth. My vow of chastity, then, bears witness to the fact that the Redeemer who offers Himself to me as Spouse, is risen and alive. He is the fullness of my life, and just as marriage completes two people, so is Jesus Christ my completion.[10]

Spousal Union with Jesus Christ

Consecrated persons who give spousal love to Christ find therein the true meaning of their lives. The Holy Father assures us again and again that Christ's own life, coming from the fullness of the Father, can be the fulfillment of each one of us personally. Thus, evangelical chastity is that special mode of love which takes us right into the heart of that most profound mystery of human existence, namely, divine love.[11]

Spousal love means an unqualified, single-hearted devotion to Christ, a devotion which is shared with no other person. Just as husband and wife through their marriage vows are reserved for each other alone, so does the vow of chastity reserve the religious for Jesus Christ alone. However, to be for the Lord and to do His work, means more than merely offering Him our time, energy and labor in apostolic activities. He wants us to offer Him our very person. This means a profound constant "yes" of a spousal order; it means loving Him above everything else. Only then can He *fully* share His "spousal" love with us.[12]

On November 16, 1978, the Holy Father addressed an international group of religious in Rome. He told them that all religious must bear witness to the primacy of God in their lives. He stressed the need to dedicate a sufficiently long period of time every day to stand before the Lord, to tell Him of their love and above all, to allow themselves to be loved by Him.[13]

To experience deeply of Christ's love and then to return it in joyful self-giving is a daily challenge. To accept this challenge means to transcend self by leaving behind all preoccupation with self. However, with our limited human powers we cannot do this of ourselves. Our only alternative, then, is to keep asking the Holy Spirit to help us. Indeed, it is the Holy Spirit who enables us to "understand" the true value of the counsel of chastity and to live it in fidelity and ever greater refinement.[14]

The gift of "understanding" given to us by the Holy Spirit comes through an inner enlightenment which transcends human intelligence. Through the activity of the Holy Spirit, the religious is able to penetrate more truly the deeper realities of the consecrated life. A new world begins to open up in which the consecrated person sees the futility of worldly values and purely self-serving attitudes. Those attachments to secular attractions which lure us away from Christ and keep us centered on self are finally "let go of." His is a demanding love which requires a constant renunciaton and a constant perseverance.

It is through the activity of the Holy Spirit, then, that religious enter into a more immediate relationship with Christ, their Spouse. In a word, the counsel of chastity is a gift of grace which liberates the human heart in a special manner so that it may be free to know and love God and thus become a source of spiritual fruitfulness for others. When chastity is lived with total and unreserved self-giving through love, and when it is marked by genuine generosity and joy, it helps others to distinguish between true love and its many counterfeits.[15]

Chastity as Witness

Today many people are tempted to live by false values. For them, living the evangelical counsel of chastity is something inconceivable. Yet, must it not be recognized that there is an amazing power at work here? Is it not true that down through the centuries the Holy Spirit has inspired thousands and thousands of men and women to forego their natural desire to marry and have a family? And have not these same people been drawn into another way of life, that of a spousal relationship with Jesus Christ? Is not this more than ample testimony that Christ is alive and active in His world? And does it not vindicate the truth that He is the fullness of life and the completion of the person who truly lives the counsel of chastity?[16]

All men and women religious have been called to a deep intimacy with our divine Spouse. The Holy Father warns us not to allow ourselves to be distracted by centers of interest other than Jesus Christ. It is the true gift of self that gives strength and joy. If an attempt is made to remove the cross and sacrifice from the consecrated life, it becomes sterile. Hence, there is no task facing the religious more urgent than that of bearing authentic witness to a personal love of Jesus Christ above all else. Indeed, this is the very heart of our religious identity.[17]

It is to Jesus Christ, then, that we religious have responded with a love that renounces all else for the sake of the kingdom, and in that renunciation we have gained all by becoming all things to all people in order to win them to Christ. Chastity, then, is above all a gift of love from Christ to each of us religious and through us to the Church.[18]

CHAPTER 6

Evangelical Poverty

By your religious profession you have freely renounced the goods of this world. Therefore, it is very important that you be detached from these goods and that you avoid, as individuals and communities, the exaggerated seeking of comforts and expensive means of living. It is impossible to live poorly without feeling the pinch of poverty. Hence, I suggest that you take a look at your lives from time to time from this point of view.

–John Paul II to Men and Women
Religious in Rome, February 2, 1987

All founders and foundresses of religious communities, and all reformers of religious life throughout the centuries believed firmly in the essential interdependence of evangelical poverty and the quality of religious life. In fact, the history of religious life shows that there were periods when the life of the counsels waxed, and there were periods when it waned; there were times when it brought forth holiness, and there were times when it fostered decadence. History thus shows that the state of religious life in each period was dependent to a great extent upon the degree to which evangelical poverty was lived.

When future generations look back on the years immediately following Vatican II, what will they see? Have the "winds of change" in the last thirty years created a situation of great disarray in the ways of viewing and practicing poverty? Perhaps this question might best be answered by answering other questions: In general do we religious today accept and live out the conciliar and post-conciliar teachings on evangelical poverty? Or more specifically: Do we really witness to the world a life lived in detachment from earthly possessions?

In past years, poverty has been seen mostly in terms of "having" or "not having." The specific regulations imposed from without did have a purpose and they did foster a genuine living of the vow. However, the danger that the practice of poverty could degenerate into the empty formalism of "keeping the law for the sake of the law" was always present. That is why the Holy Father sees the need to examine the very roots of the meaning of poverty.

A discovery of the "roots" of the meaning of this counsel, however, does not mean that the laws should be jettisoned. Rather, it means that we have to see the external law in correlation with the intrinsic nature of the counsel, and not merely as arbitrary regulations imposed from without. It means that we have to see evangelical poverty not simply as "having" or "not having" but as a mode of being.[1]

The Poverty of Christ

The more we reflect on Christ's vocation and mission, the more do we understand the meaning of our own vocation and mission. Since the Incarnate Word assumed our human nature, Jesus Christ, like us, belongs to the world of "having" and "not having." Hence, it is from Christ Himself that we learn the true meaning of evangelical poverty.

First of all, the eternal Son of God really lived the life of the poor. His birth was that of a poor person. He was born in a stable and His mother placed Him in a manger. For thirty years He lived in a family in which His father earned the daily bread by working as a carpenter and He Himself shared in this labor. In His public life Christ said of Himself: "The Son of Man has nowhere to lay his head."[2] He died on the cross as a slave, literally stripped of everything. He chose to be poor to the very end.[3]

In his second letter to the Corinthians, Paul's profound reflection on the Incarnation gives us deep insights into the mystery of Christ's poverty:

> "For you know the grace of our Lord Jesus Christ, that though he was rich, yet for your sake he became poor, so that by his poverty you might become rich."[4]

This passage from Paul's letter provides the text for the Holy Father's understanding of poverty. The Son of God is impoverished in order to be with us. His impoverishment culminates in His sacrificial death animated by His redemptive love, and our enrichment is divinity, the greatest gift possible. This is what is meant by the mystery of grace. In 2 Peter 1:3-4 we read that God has called us "to his own glory and excellence." Indeed, it is His redemptive power that empowers us "to escape from the corruption that is in the world because of passion and become partakers of the divine nature." He who is the poorest in His death on the cross is the One who enriches us infinitely with the fullness of new life. This "new life" comes to us through His resurrection. So Christ, who is the very source of all riches, had to empty Himself in order to give us all that He is.[5]

Evangelical poverty, then, is not just extraneous to redemption; it belongs to the very interior structure of the redemptive grace of Jesus Christ. The Pope writes:

> According to these words (2 Cor 8:9), poverty actually enters into the interior structure of the redemptive grace of Jesus Christ. Without poverty, it is not possible to understand the mystery of the gift of divinity to man, a gift which is accomplished precisely in Jesus Christ.[6]

Evangelical Poverty: A "Mode of Being"

As human beings our "mode of being" is spirit-in-the-world. However, since spirit alone cannot exist in the world of things, God gave us a body with built-in orientation toward things in the world. This means that things in the world are necessary for our physical, emotional, mental, social and spiritual life.

In the graced existence before the fall, things in the world were used to bring about union and the glory of God. But after the fall, our relationship to the world of things became disordered. St. John speaks of this disordered orientation as "lust of the eyes," that is, an insatiable capacity for things both material and non-material. In a situation of affluence it does not take long for that concupiscence, the lust of the eyes, to awaken in the human heart a greed for more and better possessions with the accompanying greed for the non-material such as pleasure, power, prestige, etc. Thus, abundance in any form can play into the perverse side of our nature and lead to a blinding pride which generates self-exultation, unbridled ambition, and exploitation of others. On the other hand, a simple sufficiency, or even a lack of things provide a sort of protective atmosphere in which genuineness and integrity can develop.

In the fullness of time, God sent His Son into the world to call mankind to a new mode of existence, an existence utterly beyond human existence. This is our call to holiness. Through His death and resurrection, Christ draws us into this new mode of existence, the redemptive mode.

As baptized Christians, we share in this graced existence which transforms us in our relation to the world of things. As religious, professing the vows of chastity, poverty and obedience, we commit ourselves to fashion our lives according to this new mode through sacrificial love. His call "Come follow me," simply means to live out the same sacrificial love which animated Him. In this way, evangelical poverty is really lived as a sharing in Christ's poverty.

Religious poverty, then, does not simply mean the lack of things. Nor does it mean destitution or the use of things according to their value. It does mean the redemptive orientation toward things, the going beyond what is necessary for salvation through a renunciation of not only what is sinful, but even of what is legitimate. If we open ourselves to poverty in "sacrificial love," we are drawn ever more deeply into the Paschal Mystery of Christ Himself by sharing ever more profoundly in the interior structure of the redemptive grace of Jesus Christ. This is the "paschal duality" the Holy Father speaks of where there is a gradual destruction of the "roots" of sin within (death) and a new bringing forth of the profound good in each one (resurrection).[7] With St. Paul we can say, "For him I have accepted the loss of everything ... if only I can have Christ and be given a place in him."[8]

"Poor in Spirit"

In his general audience on November 30, 1994, the Holy Father quoted Christ Himself regarding evangelical poverty: "Blessed are the poor in spirit, for theirs is the Kingdom of heaven."[9] He then explains that Christ is not referring simply to the destitute, but rather to the lowly who seek God and voluntarily choose to put themselves under His protection. Actually, the "poor in spirit" are those who do not put their trust in money or material possessions but open themselves to the realities of the Kingdom of God. It is precisely this value of poverty that Jesus praises and recommends as a life of choice.[10]

Obviously, when applied to religious life in this manner, to be "poor in spirit" calls for true humility before God. It demands total dependence upon Him. Practically, it means to free ourselves of all disordered attachments to the things of earth. Such attachments inevitably lead to a blinding pride which prevents us from recognizing the actual direction our lives may be taking. In recognition of our own human inability to become truly "poor in spirit," we turn to the Holy Spirit and beg Him to provide the strength we need to renounce earthly goods and their advantages. The Holy Spirit then forms a "spirit of poverty" within us and gives us a readiness to make the decisive act to "renounce." He thus instills a preference for the heavenly treasures which are far more valuable than material goods. In this way we develop and sustain a "taste" for a voluntary, dignified poverty renouncing everything that is not necessary.[11]

Clearly, the life of evangelical poverty is a "mode of being." The more we identify with Christ in being "poor in spirit," the more do we live ever more profoundly our redemptive mode of existence. Only then can we enrich others in a truly "redemptive way." Furthermore, it is only then that we begin to understand the richness of God's love in the emptying of Himself that we might be enriched.

Alignment with the Poor

It was Christ himself who linked the counsel of poverty not only to the need to be personally stripped of the burden of earthly possessions in order to possess the heavenly goods, but also to charity toward the poor. We saw this in His invitation to the rich young man: "Go and sell what you have and give it to the poor; you will then have treasure in heaven. After that, come and follow me."[12] Here we find Christ telling us that the preconditions for following Him are not only renouncing one's possessions, but also giving to the poor.[13]

In his addresses to religious around the world, the Holy Father repeatedly calls our attention to the needs of the poor. To a group of religious in Augsburg, Germany, on May 4, 1987, the Pope said:

> Through your poverty, you have special ties with those who are weak and without rights, those who are exploited and helpless. Place yourselves at their side and stand up for them, with courage and loyalty. Then it can be rightfully said of you: "You are poor but you make others rich; you seem to have nothing, yet everything is yours."[14]

The religious who consistently lives evangelical poverty helps others not only in a material way, but also spiritually. Jesus Himself endured material poverty to give us spiritual riches. So it was Christ Himself who inaugurated this counsel by the way He lived.

It follows, then, that the practice of evangelical poverty must be rooted in a spiritual attitude which calls forth a voluntary renunciation of unnecessary "things" in a return of one's whole being to God in service to the kingdom. It is precisely in this way that religious poverty enriches others through one's own poverty.

The Holy Father explains this beautifully in his 1984 letter to all men and women religious. He states that in the depths of this call to enrich others through one's own poverty, the hidden richness of God is transferred to the human soul in the mystery of grace. This "richness" becomes in the human soul a source for enriching others and is not comparable with any other resource of material goods. It becomes a source for bestowing gifts on others in the manner of God Himself. This giving is accomplished in the context of the mystery of Christ, who "has made us rich by his poverty."[15]

This manner of the bestowal of gifts on others is precisely what distinguished Mother Teresa of Calcutta and her followers from the ordinary social worker. What matters, then, is that poverty be really lived as a sharing in Christ's poverty.

Evangelical Poverty: A Challenge

As every religious knows, living the life of the counsels is not easy. Why is the consecrated life so difficult? The answer is simple: the disorders of concupiscence in the human heart are not removed by the profession of poverty, chastity and obedience. In fact, living the life of the counsels is a constant warfare. To live it seriously, one must engage in an unflagging struggle with self.

Evangelical poverty is difficult to live in every age, but it is especially difficult today. Consecrated religious are called to represent Christ in His poverty; yet, in a culture which values money above everything else and in a society greedy for the luxuries and enticing comforts of the day, representing Christ in His poverty is, indeed, a challenge. How can we possibly live a life of poverty in a world where affluence is so contagious? The Holy Father answers this question in his closing words to section 12 in *Redemptionis Donum*. He writes:

> Dear brothers and sisters, poor in spirit through your evangelical profession, receive into the whole of your life this salvific profile of the poverty of Christ. Day by day seek its ever greater development! Seek above all "the Kingdom of God and his righteousness" and the other things "shall be yours as well." May there be accomplished in you and through you the evangelical blessedness reserved for the poor, the poor in spirit.[16]

Here the Holy Father speaks of the "salvific profile of the poverty of Christ." This simply means that it was through Christ's own impoverishment in complete forgetfulness of self that He enriched us. The Pope urges us to receive into the whole of our humanity this "saving profile" of Christ by impoverishing ourselves in complete self-forgetfulness so that we, too, might enrich others. To the extent that we meet this challenge, we will begin to enjoy that blessedness which is reserved for the "poor in spirit."

However, knowing human nature, the Pope becomes still more specific. He urges us to immerse ourselves ever more deeply into the "salvific profile" day by day. This calls for ongoing conversion of heart. Yet, how does one go about this? Perhaps one of the Israelite sages provided the most adequate reply to this question centuries ago when he wrote:

> "Keep your heart with all vigilance; for from it flow the springs of life".[17]

Scripturally, the heart is the symbol of that inner "fountain" out of which flow the deep yearnings within us. These yearnings are the sources of our every thought, word and deed. The sacred writer was fully aware of this when he urged people to "keep watch" over their hearts. He saw the need to exercise vigilance over those ego-centered movements within, which orient our lives away from what is truly good toward that which is apparently good. If these movements are not discerned and checked, they will be externalized in ways which blind us to the deeper realities of evangelical poverty.

All through the history of religious life the practice of the daily examen in religious orders has been a constant. The test of time shows that a daily prayerful reflection on the underlying motives which prompt our behavior is essential for moving into the deeper levels of consciousness. Otherwise, we run the risk of knowing ourselves at a superficial level only. During the daily examen the Holy Spirit helps us to recognize those disordered desires and attachments which prevent us from becoming truly "poor in spirit."

Accordingly, a listening attentive heart is needed to seek the "salvific profile of the poverty of Christ" in ever greater measure. However, this "seeking" involves a day by day checkup. Does not this approach make possible the living of evangelical poverty in a world where affluence is so contagious?

Poverty as Witness

That our life of voluntary poverty may seem scandalous and

even silly to many people cannot be denied. Yet, the human person is more than what he owns. Through vowed poverty, through a life of simplicity, those who truly live evangelical poverty are more than what they do; they are more than what they achieve; they are more than what is known and perceived. Jesus Christ is their wealth! In this context, possessions, power and prestige take on secondary importance.

Vowed poverty thus speaks a language of trust in Divine Providence which is contrary to the trends in society. By following in the footsteps of Christ who was poor, we can inspire others in their search for a simpler and more authentic way of life. Our detachment from the goods of this world will act as a challenge to our contemporaries.[18]

Thus, the virtue of poverty which religious practice is rooted in a specific vow. This virtue has great relevance for religious because its faithful practice leads one to a lifestyle consistent with the vowed commitment to follow the poor and humble Christ ever more closely. Furthermore, one's personality is distinctly enriched in the liberation that comes from detachment from material things and the renunciation of the "power" that comes from their possession.

Hence, evangelical poverty should become a "mode of life" for every religious. It is an indispensable condition for "finding" God at deep levels and consequently growing in intimacy with Christ our Spouse. And is not this the prime purpose of our call to the consecrated life?

CHAPTER 7

Filial Obedience

You live lives of obedience. You have the freedom of love, since you trust in God and are certain of his love. Your criterion is the obedience of Jesus Christ: "He humbled himself, obediently accepting even death on a cross!" (Phil 2:8). With this basic attitude, you arrive at a mature obedience towards your religious superiors and Church authorities. Your obedience is above all, obedience to God; but it must be proven and incarnated in your concrete community and its rule.

—John Paul II to Women Religious and a Group of
Young Women in Augsburg, Germany, May 4, 1987

It is obedience that sets us free. However, freedom is not an absolute. It is not something just for itself. Freedom is a sort of mysterious word like "heart," "love" or "person." But as for obedience? How can it possibly set us free?

Human freedom is that fundamental orientation within us that has to do with obligation. So obedience is in a profound way related to freedom: What I ought to do or what I ought not to do. It is that built-in sense called conscience which comes from the heart of God and is written on our hearts. When we actualize the will of God in our lives, we become perfectly free. However, people tend to explain away the will of God when they do things they ought not to do.

God is the Giver of all life. It is His will, His intention to give life constantly, to increase it and to bring it to fulfillment. Since there is in every human being an orientation to life and a sense of the ought, obviously, our freedom is directed to life. Freedom, then, is a very mysterious gift by which we correspond to God's will to bring us to fullness of life in Him.

So then, we do not exist to be free to do our own will, but we do exist to be free to do God's will. After all, our freedom as created beings always lies within the greater freedom of God, our Creator. That is why the more I choose to live out the evangelical counsels, the more free do I become.[1]

The Obedience of Christ

The story of Jesus Christ does not begin with His birth in Bethlehem. It begins with His divine existence in eternity prior to His human existence in time and space. In his letter to the Philippians, Paul explains that before He entered human history, the Son had equality with God but in His humanity was willing to have it hidden:

> Christ, though he was in the form of God, did not count equality with God a thing to be grasped, but emptied himself, taking the form of a servant, being born in the likeness of men. And being found in human form he humbled himself and *became obedient* unto death, even death on a cross.[2]

Here we find Paul giving full attention to the Son's free surrender of divine authority. He freely changed His role from sovereignty over the world to obedience within it. He "humbled himself" by allowing Himself to be shaped by obedience, obedience even to the point of death. However, in this change of status, the Eternal Son of the Father did not lose anything of His divinity.

As man, Christ shared the human plight in every way except in the realm of sin. He was subject to the same laws that everyone else had to obey. He was obedient to the point of death, even death on a cross. In the words "became obedient" we have the essence of redemption, for where Adam failed, Christ succeeded:

> For as by one man's disobedience many were made sin-

ners, so by one man's obedience many will be made righteous.[3]

It is here in the obedience of Christ that we find the mystery of paschal duality. Adam's disobedience placed mankind in a condition of estrangement from God, whereas the Son's obedience unto death brings to mankind a share in eternal life. What seems to be the ultimate failure is, in fact, the maximum gain, for Christ's obedience became the means by which we are set free.[4]

The Will of the Father

As children of Adam, we tend to flee from the will of God. However, Christ searched unceasingly for the Father's will:

> "... I seek not my own will but the will of him who sent me."[5]

The Father's will was, indeed, the sole motivation of all Christ's desires. It was His very food! In doing the Father's will, He was accomplishing the Father's redemptive work:

> "My food is to do the will of him who sent me, and to accomplish his work."[6]

The spiritual struggle in Gethsemane was Christ's alone. Yet, even in the horror of this hour, Jesus knew God as His Father and placed full confidence in Him. His human nature recoiled at the very thought of the suffering He knew would come, yet He expressed His readiness to undergo maltreatment and a cruel death. It was here that Christ's obedience, rooted in the desire to please His Father, reached its zenith:

> "Abba, Father, all things are possible to thee, remove this cup from me; yet not what I will but what thou wilt."[7]

Hence, throughout Christ's entire life there was perfect unity of action between the Father and the Son:

> "He who sent me is with me; he has not left me alone, for I always do what is pleasing to him."[8]

So Jesus did not come to earth to do His own will. Rather, doing the salvific will of His Father was the whole program of His life. It was His "career," as it were. To what purpose? To bring us freedom! Through His death and resurrection He freed the human race from the domination of concupiscence, our inclination to evil due to original sin, and made possible for us a sharing in the very life of God Himself. He did this through the exercise of His own freedom:

> "I lay down my life that I may take it up again. No one takes it from me, but I lay it down of my own accord."[9]

The Counsel of Obedience

In his 1984 letter to men and women Religious, the Pope proceeds to show how the counsel of obedience draws the religious into the realm of Christ's own redemptive power. Those who respond to the call to follow Christ, follow Him who freed humanity from slavery to sin. He did this through an obedience which took Him to an incredibly cruel death. By fulfilling this counsel, the religious gains a special sharing in the obedience of that "One alone" whose obedience brought us redemption.

The Holy Father further explains that those of us who decide to live according to this counsel are placed in a unique way between the "mystery of sin and the mystery of justification and salvific grace." He reminds us that we are in this "place" with all the sinful background of our human nature. We, too, inherit the "pride of life" with all the sinful tendencies to dominate rather than to serve. However, through our profession of the evangelical counsel of obedience, we freely choose to imitate the obedience of the Redeemer in a special way. In living out this counsel, we gradually become transformed into the likeness of Christ and we participate in a specific way in His redemptive mission.

The Pope insists that this counsel cannot be lived without humility, which simply means to be authentic, to be what we profess to be. By our vow of obedience, then, we have taken upon ourselves the duty of a particular reference to Christ, obedient unto death.

The Holy Father further urges that we who profess evangelical obedience reflect on Mary and her role in the redemption of the world:

> "Behold I am the handmaid of the Lord; let it be done unto me according to your word."[10]

These are the words of obedient love which led Mary to the foot of the cross and also to the joy of the resurrection. This is the meaning of that mysterious paschal duality involved in our profession of the counsel of obedience.[11]

Religious Authority

The structure of religious life reflects the Christian hierarchy of which the head is Christ Himself. These structures require a form of government that expresses a particular form of religious authority. This authority does not derive from the members themselves; rather, it is conferred by the Church when the institute is established and the constitutions are approved. This is the authority which is invested in superiors for the duration of their term of office.

In an address to the Superiors General of Women Religious in Rome on November 14, 1979, the Holy Father drew from the Vatican II documents for much of what he shared. He had numerous reminders and exhortations for superiors regarding their responsibility. In carrying out their duties, religious superiors themselves should be docile to God's will. They should respect and listen to their subjects while retaining their authority to make decisions.

The Holy Father realizes that the exercise of authority in a spirit of service and love for all the members is not only a vital task, but also a difficult one. It calls for no little courage and dedication. Indeed, superiors are responsible for the souls entrusted to them. The Pope stressed that it is not only harsh authoritarianism, but also misguided permissiveness which destroys true community life. Both are deviations which are equally harmful not only to individual religious but also to the community at large and to the Church in general.[12]

In this same address to major superiors the Holy Father reminded them of the indispensable need of a deep love for the Church. He maintained that faithfulness to Christ can never be separated from faithfulness to the Church. In order to carry out a truly effective apostolate, individual members under the leadership of the superior, must assume a position of humble and constant docility to the teachings of the Church's Magisterium. They are to follow the pastoral directives of the successors of Peter and of the bishops in communion with him. As a matter of fact, this ecclesial dimension is absolutely essential for a correct understanding of religious life.[13]

The Holy Father likewise urged superiors to take to heart his exhortation for fervent and persevering prayer. He said that the life story of every religious is centered on a nuptial love for Christ to whom she gives her whole life. Thus, molded by His Spirit, she will adopt His sentiments, His ideals and His mission of charity and salvation. Then, quoting from an address he gave to priests and men and women religious in Ireland, the Holy Father said:

> No movement in religious life has any importance unless it also be movement inward to the "still center" of your existence where Christ is. It is not what you *do* that matters most, but what you *are* as persons consecrated to God.[14]

Superiors, however, do not exercise authority in isolation. Each must have the assistance of a council whose members collaborate with the superior according to the norms stated in the constitution. They help by offering their consultative or deliberative vote according to ecclesiastical law and the constitutions of the institute. They do not exercise authority by right of office as superiors do.[15]

Supreme authority in an institute is also exercised by a general chapter while it is in session. It should represent the entire institute and should be a true sign of its unity and love. It exercises supreme authority in accordance with common law and the norms of the constitution. Delegates to the general chapter should be mindful of the grave responsibility they have before the congregation and the Church.

The foremost duty of the general chapter is to protect the patrimony of the institute and to promote suitable renewal in accord with this patrimony. It also elects the supreme moderator, treats major business matters and publishes norms which all are to obey.[16]

Religious Obedience
Religious obedience originates in the obedience of Christ

whose duty and joy it was to carry out the Father's plan. His obedience to the Father, however, did not deter Him from being obedient to human intermediaries. He was not only obedient to Mary and Joseph, but He also obeyed all lawful human authority. Hence, Jesus is always the model of all religious in living their vow of obedience.

On the day of our final profession, we committed ourselves to the authority prescribed and designated by our respective constitutions. This commitment extends to us Christ's own commitment to the Father. Obedience, then, does not bring about the loss of dignity; rather, it brings us to an ennobling maturity by enabling us to grow in the freedom of the children of God.

Accordingly, moved by the Holy Spirit, we have voluntarily subjected ourselves in faith to those who hold God's place, our religious superiors. However, difficulties that sometimes arise in the matter of obedience are often due to the failure to see the divine representative in a human person. That is why it should be kept in mind that religious obedience is not simply submission to human authority; rather, it means submission to the divine will expressed in the will of the superior. This has to be a matter of faith.

In his general audience on December 7, 1994, the Holy Father spoke on evangelical obedience. He said that on occasion it may seem that the path indicated by a superior may not be the best one for one's self-fulfillment or the use of one's talents. He also mentioned that even if a decision is deemed to be unwise, provided the directive is not contrary to the law of God or the rule, a judgment based on faith accepts the mystery of God's will. Many religious in looking back over difficult years can now testify that "All things work together unto good."[17] It was a mature understanding of obedience that prompted them to obey.

Obviously, it is through our vow of obedience that we are taken far beyond any personal destiny. The sacrifice of one's will out of love yields an abundant fruit of salvation for the whole world. In other words, through our obedience we share in a special way in the work of universal redemption.

Without question, the obedience which marks those of us who profess the consecrated life is, indeed, a continuation of the obedience of Christ to the Father. It gives us the freedom to follow Christ in seeking exclusively the works of the Father. Above all, it draws us into the immediacy of the Father's plan of salvation and gives us the capacity to help bring it to fruition.

A Power That Threatens?

The temptation to see the will of God as a power that threatens runs through the whole of human history. It leads to all the perversions of obedience where human authority is seen as alien and a threat to one's freedom and independence. It is seen to be diminishing and demeaning.

For those of us who are religious, this distorted image of authority may affect our obedience to the Pope, the Magisterium, religious superiors and the constitutions. If this is my image of authority, the only way I can face God's will is in some way to undermine authority by making myself superior to it. This can be done in various ways.

I can undermine authority by refusing to cooperate; this gives me a feeling of superiority. Or I can fragment the will of God by causing division; this, too, gives me a sense of superiority. Or I can pretend that God's will is not there by resorting to false democratization or consensus. But this is an illusion, for there is no way I can get rid of the will of God. Or I can simply reject His will by falling prey to the clutches of erroneous teaching or the snare of popular but false trends. But actually, the will of God is beyond the reach of human rejection.[18]

Obedience and Freedom

When we religious pronounced our vows, we were not stripped of the frailties of human nature. Due to the fact that we inherit the "pride of life" from our first parents, we continue to be subject to "all the selfish tendencies to dominate rather than to serve."[19] In other words, the radical temptation to see the will of God as a power that threatens may at times present itself to us.

However, our hope and desire to live out our consecrated life ever more fully should not be shaken, for "Christ has set our freedom free from the domination of concupiscence!"[20] In his 1984 letter to all men and women religious, the Holy Father reminds us that through our vow of obedience we have freely chosen to be transformed in the likeness of Christ *"who, by an obedience* which carried him to death on the Cross, redeemed humanity and made it holy."[21] He accomplished this through the exercise of His own freedom. He laid down His life *of "his own accord."* He made the human decision to do the Father's will. Here in Christ's obedience we find the mystery of paschal duality, death/resurrection. It is in my vow of obedience that I find a particular way of living out this mystery in my own life. This is a profound reality!

When I "lay down" my own personal preferences of my own accord, and then take up my life again in obedience, I live out this mystery in union with Christ. Just as Christ's own redemptive obedience unto death cleanses the world of corruption and death and makes available the fullness of life in the resurrection, so does obedience in the life of a consecrated person free one from deep-seated pride and at the same time it enriches the spousal relationship of that person with Christ. Religious thus become effective in the great drama of redemption to the extent that the Paschal Mystery of obedience is reproduced in our lives. This role in the life of each religious pervades our whole vocation in the Church.[22]

On September 17, 1987, the Holy Father addressed a large group of men and women religious in San Francisco. He told them that it is through obedience that we religious are intimately united with Jesus in seeking always to fulfill the Father's will. He said that such obedience unlocks in us the full measure of Christian freedom which enables us to serve God's people with selfless and unselfish devotion.[23]

Essential to a correct understanding of the counsel of obedience is a correct understanding of Christian freedom. In a word, the basic disorientation which holds the human heart captive is known as "the pride of life." However, our day-by-day faithfulness to our vow of obedience not only frees us from our illusory and self-serving ways but also transforms us into the likeness of Christ Himself. So, there is really no contradiction between obedience and freedom. In fact, it is obedience that sets us free — and thus enables us to enter into the redemptive work of Jesus Christ at deep levels.

CHAPTER 8

Religious Life in the Church

The evangelical counsels constitute a gift of God which the Church has received from the Lord and which by his grace she always safeguards.

—*Lumen Gentium*, 43

In the Fall of 1987, Pope John Paul II made his second pastoral visit to the United States. At an evening meeting with 3,000 men and women religious in San Francisco, the Holy Father was interrupted by applause 15 times during his address. Among other topics fundamental to religious life, the Pope stated that the Second Vatican Council remains the necessary point of reference and the guiding light for a profound discernment of Christ's will for His Church at this moment of her life.[1]

Throughout his entire pontificate, Pope John Paul II has been solicitous for the renewal of the Church according to the council. In his addresses to religious he has repeatedly called our attention to the wealth of conciliar and post-conciliar teaching on the Church itself, as well as the ecclesial dimension of the consecrated life, the inestimable value of public witness to the Church and the nature of our apostolic work in the Church.

In reflecting carefully on *Redemptionis Donum*, we note that the Holy Father gets to the heart of our faith and to the heart of religious life. The Pope begins the final chapter of this apostolic exhortation by inviting the entire Church to renew her love for Christ. He points out to us religious that, as consecrated men and women, we occupy a special place in the universal community of the People of God, and in every local community.

The Holy Father becomes more specific when he states that within the Church, consecrated persons have a special role in directing the love of the whole body toward the Spouse, the Head of the body. Furthermore, he tells us that if we love the Spouse who is the Head, we will also love His body, the Church, in its entirety: the People of God and the hierarchical structure initiated by Christ Himself.

Here, too, we find the Pope giving special emphasis to the fact that the Church, the Body of Christ, expects religious to think with the Church and always to act in union with her in conformity with the teachings of the Magisterium. He states that love for the Church in all its aspects is inseparable from religious life.[2]

What Is the Church?

The Church is a gift from above, a mystery of faith. Just as the Father gave everything to the Son, so the Son, through the Holy Spirit, has given everything to the Church. Actually, the Church is a sacrament. She is not only a sign of intimate union with God, but she is, in fact, the instrument for achieving this union. It is in the Church that God desires to encounter humanity and humanity longs to encounter God. In other words, the Church is the meeting point between God and man.[3]

In order that we might more fully understand the indispensable "connection" between religious life and the Church, the Pope frequently stresses the necessity for religious to have a correct and complete understanding of the Church as the council fathers, under the guidance of the Holy Spirit, set forth in *Lumen Gentium*. He likewise urges us to meditate on the rich conciliar and post-conciliar teaching of the Church concerning the consecrated life. He claims that these teachings must become better known by making them the object of our personal and communal reflection.

During the Mass celebrated in the cathedral of Mexico City on January 29, 1979, the Holy Father delivered an insightful and moving homily in which he summoned those present to an intelligent and staunch loyalty to the Church today. He said:

> The Pope who visits you, expects from you a generous and noble effort to know the Church better and better. The Second Vatican Council wished to be above all, a Council on the Church. Take in your hands the documents of the Council, especially *Lumen Gentium*; study them with loving attention, with the spirit of prayer, to discover what the Spirit wished to say about the Church. In this way you will be able to realize that there is not — as some people claim — a "new Church," different or opposed to the "old church," but that the Council wished to reveal more clearly the one Church of Jesus Christ, with new aspects, but still the same in its essence.[4]

Lumen Gentium, known as the *Dogmatic Constitution on the Church*, was promulgated by Pope Paul VI on November 21, 1964. The document begins with these words: "Christ is the light of humanity." Since Christ is the light of all people, it was the heart-felt desire of the council fathers to bring this light to all nations. Hence, the council set out to present and further clarify the nature and universal mission of the Church in the light of tradition and the earlier councils.

The Church is, indeed, an inner mystical supernatural reality. Yet, at the same time, she is an external, visible, tangible and juridical reality. The Church, then, has its divine element and its human element, its spiritual element and its tangible element. In the Church we find light, strength, and the true meaning of all of our life. In fact, she embraces our entire existence, our every activity and expression of personality. Furthermore, it is in the Church that we meet our brethren, those whom the Father is also calling. But above all, this takes place only because it is in the Church that we encounter Christ personally, and through Him, we share in the intimate life of the Trinity.[5]

All people are called to this union in Christ who is the Light of the World; we all come forth from Him; we live through Him and our whole life is directed towards Him. Hence, the universal Church is seen to be a people brought into unity from the unity of the Father, the Son and the Holy Spirit.

The Council made clear that this is the one, holy, catholic and apostolic Church which Christ, after His resurrection, entrusted to Peter's pastoral care. At the same time, He commissioned Peter and the other apostles to extend and direct it. Furthermore, it was Christ's intent that this Church would last until the end of time and that it would be the indispensable conveyer and support of truth in the world.

Chapter IV of *Lumen Gentium* is titled "Religious." Here in compelling and explicit language the council fathers tell about our distinct relationship to the Church. The more fully we understand the Church, the more truly will we live out our vocation in the Church as consecrated religious.

Ecclesial Dimension of Religious Life

In *Lumen Gentium* we read that our religious consecration binds us to the Church in a special way. While the Christian life is linked with the Church in the sacrament of Baptism, the religious state involves a special bond with Christ and, consequently, it involves a special tie with the Church. In fact, it is in the Church that we find the reason for our life as a religious.[6]

When we pronounced our vows, we incorporated ourselves into the whole of the Church's life. Through our superiors, we entrusted ourselves to the Church, offering her all our faculties and gifts of nature and grace. Through her ecclesial representative, the Church received our vows and made them her own. Thus, our life has been taken up by the Church in a way that is altogether special, because our offering, which was accepted by the Church, is united to that of Christ.[7] This concept is presented in *Lumen Gentium* in these words:

> She herself (the Church), in virtue of her God-given authority, receives the vows of those who profess this form of life, asks aid and grace for them from God in her public prayer, commends them to God and bestows on them a spiritual blessing, associating their self-offering with the sacrifice of the Eucharist.[8]

In reflecting on the Holy Father's many addresses to religious, we frequently find him pleading with us to deepen our ecclesial awareness so that we might relate to God, to ourselves and to our neighbor in a truly Christ-like way. We are integrated into the Church and her mystery through our personal commitment to Christ. To the degree that we actually do commit ourselves to Him, to that degree do we contribute to the spiritual enrichment of others. This ecclesial dimension is essential for the consecrated life and is significant for apostolic fruitfulness.

On October 7, 1979, the Holy Father addressed a large group of women religious in the Shrine of the Immaculate Conception in Washington, D.C. He explained that religious consecration not only deepens personal commitment to Christ, but also strengthens one's relationship to the Church. Indeed, religious life is a distinctive manner of living in the Church. Accordingly, Christ must always be first in the life of every religious. This means that He must enjoy the first place in our minds and hearts, for it is only in this way that we can conform our lives more closely to Him. The Holy Father further stated that faithfulness to Christ, especially in religious life, can never be separated from faithfulness to the Church.[9]

On February 1, 1985, the Holy Father addressed the clergy, religious and laity in Lima, Peru. He told those involved in Christian education that Christians have a right to demand from the consecrated person a sincere allegiance and obedience to the commandments of Christ and His Church. He said:

> Live and inculcate always a deep love for the Church, and a loyal allegiance to all her teachings. Never be bearers of uncertainties, but rather of the certainties of faith. Always transmit the truths that the Magisterium proclaims, not ideologies that pass away.[10]

Again and again we find the Holy Father reiterating the Council teachings regarding the purpose of religious life in the Church. He reminds us that the consecrated life is not on the level of institutional structures, but rather in the line of charisms. More especially, however, it is rooted in the dynamism of that primary vocation of the Church, namely, holiness. To a large group of men religious in Sao Paulo on July 3, 1980, the Pope said:

> The first reason for which a Christian becomes a Religious is not to assume a post, a responsibility, or a task in

the Church, but to sanctify himself. This is his task and his responsibility, "and all these things shall be his as well." This is his service for the Church: the Church needs this school of holiness, in order to realize concretely her own vocation of holiness.[11]

From September to December of 1994, the Pope's general audience talks were devoted to catechesis on the consecrated life. On September 28, he quoted the Council in these words:

[T]he religious state, which is constituted by the profession of the evangelical counsels, although it does not belong to the hierarchical structure of the Church, does, however, belong *unquestionably* to her life and holiness.[12]

The Holy Father then added his own thoughts regarding this teaching:

This adverb — *unquestionably* — means that all the blows that can disturb the Church's life will never be able to eliminate the consecrated life characterized by the profession of the evangelical counsels. This state of life will endure as an essential element of the Church's holiness. According to the Council, this is an unshakable truth.[13]

Public Witness

On February 17, 1981, the Holy Father met with a group of men religious in the beautiful cathedral in Manila. He began his talk by expressing his gratitude to them for their presence in the Church and for their collaboration in the Church's mission of proclaiming the Gospel of our Lord Jesus Christ. He then proceeded to tell them that the world needs the public witness of religious life and that their witness is a vital contribution to the mission of the Church. Then quoting from his predecessor, Pope Paul VI, the Holy Father said, "Modern man listens more willingly to witnesses than to teachers, and if he does listen to teachers, it is because they are witnesses."[14]

Religious life is always a visible sign of the Church. As religious, we bear witness to the world that the Lord is truly worthy of being loved above all things and followed with total dedication. Hence, care must be taken that the proper characteristics of the consecrated life be in evidence at all times.

Today's world certainly needs witness of the consecrated life. It is most obvious that our contemporary culture makes it easy for people to forget God, to make idols of pleasure, material possessions and the exercise of power. However, none of these can bring lasting happiness; nor can they give to anyone the true meaning of life. Religious testify to the world that it is by "losing one's life" that they "find it" in abundance. Thus, a life of poverty, chastity and obedience willingly embraced and faithfully lived, contradicts the accepted wisdom of the world about the meaning of life.

Many times in addressing religious, the Holy Father reminds us that the world needs religious who are willing to be signs of contradiction; not the contradiction of truth, but of error. He maintains that the first witness should be that of filial adherence and unfailing faithfulness to the Church. Such generous and loving adherence to the authentic Magisterium of the Church is a solid guarantee of the fruitfulness of our apostolates as well as an indispensable condition for the proper interpretation of the "signs of the times."[15]

The Holy Father frequently reminds religious that community life is closely linked with the mystery of the Church. He urges that good community life be nurtured so that it will be a precious means of mutual help, personal growth and fruitful witness to others. He further claims that as members of the Church with a special consecrated vocation, our witness of the common life constitutes in itself an effective means of sanctification, precisely through our detachment from material things and worldly values.

Furthermore, over the years the Pope has told religious repeatedly that our witness is strengthened by manifesting our consecration in a visible way through the wearing of a religious habit. He says that people have a right to know who we are. He points out that this is a silent but strong and eloquent testimony to the modern city where the sense of the sacred is all but lost. He claims that our modern secularized society needs to find people inspired by faith and love who fearlessly give public witness by living out the radical demands of the Gospel.

We know that clothes are not only functional for warmth, but they are also a sign, a statement to others. In religious life they can be a statement of preference for secular values or a manifestation of consecration and a commitment to poverty. Obviously, clothes themselves, like our words, are always a statement to others.

On another occasion, the Pope became yet more explicit in this regard. He told a large group of priests and men and women religious not to hesitate to be recognizable in the streets as men and women who have consecrated their lives to God, and who have given up everything worldly to follow Christ. He stated that contemporary men and women set value on the visible signs of the consecration of their lives. Furthermore, people need such signs and reminders of God in the modern secular city. He exhorted these priests and religious not to help the trend toward "taking God off the streets" by adopting secular modes of dress and behavior themselves.[16] Pope John Paul II insists that these and other ways of witnessing are invaluable signs needed today by all of humanity. Without the love behind these various forms of witness, the presence of Christ would be reduced in the world. Consequently, our witness as religious is at the very heart of the Church.

That our lives can be immensely powerful witnesses to Christ's love is manifested in the lives of both Pope John Paul II and Mother Teresa of Calcutta. Not only the Catholic laity, but also non-Catholics and even non-Christians find in them a symbol of what humanity should be like. This kind of witness gives proof that the redemption has truly taken place.

As religious, then, we are called to be a sign of God. Our witness should testify that He is the center and source of life for all people. This means that our ideals, values, convictions and daily living should manifest that we are at the service of God and His interests. Unless our witness is clear and consistent, our apostolate will lose its power to evangelize.

The Meaning of Apostolate

Today, the understanding of "apostolate" is often confined to a very narrow and even secular meaning. However, in

Redemptionis Donum we find the Pope clarifying this misconception. His explanation is definite and clear-cut. He writes that our specific mission "is in harmony with the mission of the apostles whom the Lord sent 'to the whole world' to 'teach all nations.'"[17]

Since the Church, through the apostles, takes her origin in the mission of the Son, she is missionary by her very nature. Our service in the Church, then, is actually an extension of the mission of Christ to Whom we have dedicated our lives. We labor in the name of the Church, and the Church labors in us. Consequently, it is not we ourselves we are to put forward, but it is Christ Jesus, our Lord. Our apostolic fruitfulness is totally dependent upon this.

In his many addresses to men and women religious, the Holy Father advises us to remember always that the specific and ultimate aim of all apostolic service is to lead the men and women of today to communion with the Most Holy Trinity. However, in order to do this, a preliminary step is essential. He tells us that the first field of our apostolate is our own personal life. In other words, our first apostolic duty is our own sanctification.

On February 17, 1981, the Holy Father addressed a group of women religious in Manila. He told them that their first responsibility is to strive to live a life hidden with Christ in God. In this way, they intensify their personal and communal familiarity with the principal Source of apostolic and charitable activity. Only in this way will we religious share intimately in that mission which takes its origin from the Father. The Pope warned that a constant danger for apostolic workers is to become so involved in their own work for the Lord, as to forget the Lord of all work.[18]

At times the Holy Father puzzles over the gigantic problem of the large number of Catholics who live outside the Church. He acknowledges that there are many factors responsible for this. At the same time, he asks whether or not these Christians have had sufficient and authentic evangelizing, and he questions the witness of many of the evangelizers. That is why he reminds us repeatedly not to let the "salt" of the Gospel become insipid through secularizing practices and attitudes. He warns against adopting a socio-political behavior determined by criteria that are not always evangelical.

And yet, the Pope always encourages us to invest all our

natural and supernatural talents in contemporary evangelization. He maintains that the only way to do this is to be present in the world without being of the world.

On September 3, 1987, in the historic Cathedral of San Fernando in San Antonio, Texas, a large group of seminarians and candidates for the religious life eagerly waited to see and hear Pope John Paul II. Regarding their future apostolates, he told them that there will be a thousand ways in which the Church will call them into service in her mission for the Kingdom of God. Then he went on to say:

> She (the Church) *needs your work* and everything that you can do for the Gospel. But above all, the Church needs what you are; *she needs you*: men and women consecrated to God living in union with Christ, living in union with the Church, striving after the perfection of love. Why? *Because of the holiness of God!* Dear brothers and sisters: *what you do is important, but what you are is even more important* — more important for the world, more important for the Church, more important for Christ.[19]

Meeting groups of consecrated men and women religious on his apostolic journeys always gave the Holy Father great joy. His constant endeavor has always been to help all of us religious to know our proper place in the Church. He invariably insists that we "belong undeniably to the life and holiness of the Church."[20]

Accordingly, it cannot be questioned that our Christian dignity depends principally not on what we do in service to the Church and the world, but on what we are: namely, consecrated followers of Jesus Christ.

EPILOGUE

A call from God can capture anyone, anywhere, at any time in life. Such a call transcends the imagination; it baffles the human mind; it is unmerited; it is unearned. What, then, determines the divine choice? One word: love!

[T]he Lord set his heart upon you and chose you (Deut. 7:7).

Those of us who are living the consecrated life have received a special call from Christ Himself. In my own call God looked at me with love. He did not look at me and leave me where I was. No, His love pursued me until I became conscious of it and turned and looked at Him. Christ beckoned and I followed. Yes, I left all and followed Him.

It was thus that God set me aside, as it were, to live an unusual life, a life that demands that I do more than just what is necessary for salvation. I have been called to follow Christ by living radically the evangelical counsels of chastity, poverty and obedience. My free and full response to this special call requires an undivided heart. In the voluntary gift of my total self to Christ, I enter into a spousal relationship with Him. I must always remember that my call to the consecrated life is a mystery. It can never be fully understood in merely human terms because it is the work of the Holy Spirit.

The counsel of chastity is addressed in a particular way to the human heart. It means a single-hearted devotion to Christ which is shared with no other person. It gives freedom to enter into the redemptive plan of God by serving others without condition and without discrimination.

Poverty frees the heart from slavish and unrestrained attach-

73

ment to created things. A spiritual attitude toward poverty involves the renunciation of all unnecessary "things" in a return of one's whole being to God. Thus, evangelical poverty leads the religious into the realm of redemptive impoverishment by which others are enriched.

Obedience sets us free, free to do God's will. Human freedom always lies within the greater freedom of God, our Creator. The more we live out the will of God from moment to moment, the more are we set free from those hindrances that hold us back from true freedom. Indeed, it is the counsel of obedience that liberates the human heart from the "pride of life" and frees the religious to grow in the likeness of Christ.

In *Lumen Gentium* we read that our religious consecration binds us to the Church in a special way. In fact, the evangelical counsels are a gift to the Church from God Himself and it is through the Holy Spirit that she interprets and safeguards them. So it is in the Church that we find the reason for our life as a religious.

The updating and renewal of the consecrated life was a matter of great concern for the council fathers. Vatican II asked for an adaptation and renewal of the consecrated life, a renewal which would free religious of outdated encumbrances and practices and foster a desire for the deeper realities of the life of the counsels. Renewal was to be the work of the Holy Spirit and not the "spirit of self."

Immediately after the council, many congregations entered into the task of renewing with great hope and energy. However, the secularizing processes at work in society do not leave untouched those consecrated to God. Because we live in a time of chaos, of spiritual disorientation and confusion, there are many liberal and secularizing forces all around us. Without a doubt, all religious have a deep yearning for God. Yet we, too, are subject to the temptations coming from a "laid back" and loose-ended culture. Consequently, in recent years, less attention has been given to Vatican II renewal.

In many instances, the deeper realities of the life of the counsels have been lost sight of due to the replacement of authentic renewal with false renewal. An effort to relax the lifestyle of religious life has led to the mitigation or dropping of purposeful and meaningful rules, customs and practices with the consequent compromise, more or less, of the deeper realities of the consecrated life.

On May 12, 1985, Pope John Paul II addressed a large group of religious in Utrecht. There he expressed concern regarding the drop in vocations. Then he asked, "To what is this due?" He answered his own question in these words: "Undoubtedly the cultural changes of our age provide part of the explanation, but one must think also of the process of secularization which affects religious life."[1] He then noted that there is a slow but relentless suppression of the specific and visible features of the consecrated life. He further stated that a certain "middle-class" outlook has weakened the search for the "one thing necessary" to which the religious life must bear witness.

Since the beginning of his pontificate, the Holy Father has manifested great concern regarding the renewal of the consecrated life. He maintains that this renewal in the spirit of Vatican II is essential if religious are to live out their special call to follow Christ by the authentic living of the evangelical counsels. He stresses the need for the world to see that religious are willing to be signs of contradiction, not the contradiction of truth, but of error.

In studying the letters and allocutions addressed to men and women religious around the world between the years 1978 and 1998, we find that the Holy Father himself draws unceasingly from the conciliar and post-conciliar teachings. He often expresses the wish that Vatican II teachings become better known, meditated upon, absorbed and lived by religious, both personally and communally. Then, too, we find him constantly encouraging religious to continue along the path of authentic and profound renewal which the Holy Spirit, through the Second Vatican Council, has marked out for all religious orders.

Indeed, it is in the renewal of religious life in the true spirit of Vatican II, and in this renewal alone, that religious life will again flourish in this country and in the world. We repeatedly find the Holy Father pleading with religious not to lose heart. He keeps reminding us to look to the future with confidence in complete reliance on the fidelity of God and the power of His grace.

END NOTES

Chapter 1

1. Deut 7:7.
2. Gen 12:1.
3. Ex 3:10.
4. Is 6:8.
5. Jer 1:5.
6. Ex 3:5.
7. Is 6:1.
8. Is 6:3-4.
9. Gen 12:4.
10. Is 6:8.
11. Ex 4:10.
12. Jer 1:6.
13. Jer 1:7-8.
14. Mk 3:13.
15. Mt 16:24.
16. Mk 10:17.
17. Mk 10:19.
18. Mt 19:20.
19. cf. Mk 10:21.
20. Jn 3:16.
21. cf. John Paul II, *Redemptionis Donum*, 3.
22. cf. *John Paul II Speaks to Religious*, Vol. 8, 1993-1994, No. 207.

Chapter 2

1. Mt 19:29.
2. Mt 17:5.
3. Jn 6:44.

4. Jn. 17:9.
5. Jn 15:9.
6. cf. John Paul II, *Vita Consecrata,* 15-16.
7. *Ibid.*, 19.
8. *RD,* 3.
9. 1 Cor 6:19-20.
10. *RD,* 3.
11. *VC,* 18.
12. Mt 16:24.
13. St. Teresa of Avila, *The Collected Works of St. Teresa of Avila,* Vol. One, trans. Kavanaugh, O.C.D., and Rodriguez, O.C.D., Washington, D.C., ICS Publications, 1987, p.148.
14. Lk 9:62.
15. cf. *John Paul II Speaks to Religious,* Vol. 8, 1993-1994, No. 217.
16. Mt 19:21.
17. cf. *RD*, 4.
18. Mt 10:39.
19. cf. *RD*, 5.
20. *Ibid.*

Chapter 3

1. cf. Bishop John R. Sheets, S.J., "The Primordial Mystery of Consecration," *Review for Religious* (Sept./Oct., 1985), pp. 641-643.

2. *RD*, 4.

3. *Lumen Gentium, 3.*

4. Adrienne Von Speyr, "Meditations on John," *The Farewell Discourses, Vol. 3* (San Francisco: Ignatius Press 1987), p. 354.

5. Jn 20-21.

6. *John Paul II Speaks to Religious,* Vol. 8, 1993-1994, No. 198.

7. *Ibid.,* No. 102.

8. Lk 4:16-18.

9. Lk. 4:21.

10. cf. *John Paul II Speaks to Religious,* Vol. 8, 1993-1994, No. 102.

11. Jn 17-19.

12. cf. *VC*, 22.

13. Jn 6:38.

14. *John Paul II Speaks to Religious,* Vol. 8, 1993-1994, No. 102.

15. *RD*, 7.

16. *Ibid.*

17. Is 43:1.

18. cf. *John Paul II Speaks to Religious,* Vol. 6, 1989-1990, No. 367.

19. *Ibid.*

20. cf. *RD*, 8.

21. Heb 10:5-7.

22. cf. *RD*, 8.

23. *John Paul II Speaks to Religious*, Vol. 9, 1995-1996, No. 52.

Chapter 4

1. *RD*, 9.

2. *John Paul II Speaks to Religious*, Vol. 4, 1985-1986, No. 27.

3. 1 Jn. 2:15-17.

4. *RD*, 9.

5. *Ibid.*

6. cf. *John Paul II Speaks to Religious*, Vol. 3, 1983-1984, No. 12.

7. *RD*, 10.

8. *Ibid.*

9. cf. *VC*, 24.

10. Rom 8:19-21.

11. *RD*, 9.

Chapter 5

1. Jn 1:18.

2. cf. *RD*, 11.

3. Hos 2:19-20.

4. Sheets, John, S.J., Retreat notes on *Redemptionis Donum.*

5. *Ibid.*

6. Mt 19:12.

7. cf. *RD*, 11.

8. cf. *Ibid.*

9. 1 Cor 7:32, 34.

10. Sheets, S.J., Retreat Notes.

11. cf. *John Paul II Speaks to Religious*, Vol. 5, 1987-

1988, No. 92.

12. Sheets, Retreat Notes.

13. cf. *John Paul II Speaks to Religious*, Vol. 1, 1978-1980, No. 21.

14. Sheets, Retreat Notes.

15. cf. *John Paul II Speaks to Religious,* Vol. 4, 1985-1986, No. 87.

16. Sheets, Retreat Notes.

17. cf. *John Paul II Speaks to Religious,* Vol. 6, 1989-1990, No. 393.

18. cf. *John Paul II Speaks to Religious*, Vol. 4, 1985-1986, Vol. 4, No. 410.

Chapter 6

1. Sheets, Retreat Notes.

2. Lk 9:58.

3. cf. *John Paul II Speaks to Religious*, Vol. 8, 1993-1994, No. 248.

4. 2 Cor 8:9.

5. Sheets, Retreat Notes.

6. cf. *RD*, 12.

7. Sheets, Retreat Notes.

8. Phil 3:8.

9. Mt 5:3.

10. cf. *John Paul II Speaks to Religious*, Vol. 8, 1993-1994, No. 249.

11. cf. *John Paul II Speaks to Religious*, Vol. 9, 1995-1996, No. 218.

12. Mk 10:21.

13. cf. *John Paul II Speaks to Religious*, Vol. 8, 1993-1994, No. 246.

14. cf. *John Paul II Speaks to Religious*, Vol. 5, 1987-1988, No. 95.

15. cf. *RD*, 12.

16. *RD*, 12.

17. Prov 4:23.

18. Sheets, Retreat Notes.

Chapter 7

1. Sheets, Retreat Notes.

2. Phil 2:6-8.

3. Rom 5:19.

4. cf. *RD*, 13.

5. Jn 5:30.

6. Jn 4:34.

7. Mk 14:36.

8. Jn 8:29.

9. Jn 10:17-18.

10. Lk 1:38.

11. cf. *RD*, 13.

12. cf. *John Paul II Speaks to Religious*, Vol. 1, 1977-1978, No. 265.

13. *Ibid.,* No. 259.

14. *Ibid.,* No. 253.

15. cf. *Essential Elements in the Church's Teaching on Religious Life,* n. 50.

16. cf. *Code of Canon Law, 631.*

17. Rom 8:28.

18. Sheets, Retreat Notes.

19. cf. *RD*, 13.

20. John Paul II, *Veritatis Splendor,* 103.

21. *RD*, 13.

22. Sheets, Retreat Notes.

23. cf. *John Paul II Speaks to Religious,* Vol. 5, 1987-1988, No. 169.

Chapter 8

1. cf. *John Paul II Speaks to Religious*, Vol. 5, 1987-1988, No. 170.

2. cf. *RD*, 14.

3. cf. Rev. Elio Gambari, S.M.M., *Renewal in Religious Life*, (Boston: Daughters of St. Paul, 1967), p. 59.

4. *Visible Signs of the Gospel*: Messages of John Paul II on Consecrated Life (Boston: Daughters of St. Paul, 1980), pp. 57-58.

5. cf. Rev. Elio Gambari, S.M.M., *Journey Toward Renewal* (Boston: Daughters of St. Paul, 1968), pp. 66-67.

6. cf. *LG*, 44.

7. cf. Gambari, *Journey Toward Renewal*, pp. 67-68.

8. *LG*, 45.

9. cf. *John Paul II Speaks to Religious*, Vol. 1, 1978-1980, No. 231.

10. *John Paul II Speaks to Religious*, Vol. 4, 1985-1986, No. 46.

11. *Ibid., No.* 660.

12. *LG*, 44.

13. *John Paul II Speaks to Religious*, Vol. 8, 1993-1994, No. 185.

14. cf. *John Paul II Speaks to Religious*, Vol. 2, 1981-1982, No. 37.

15. *Visible Signs of the Gospel*, Messages of John Paul II on Consecrated Life, pp. 232-233.

16. cf. *John Paul II Speaks to Religious*, Vol. 1, 1978-1980, No. 192.

17. cf. *RD*, 15.

18. cf. *John Paul II Speaks to Religious*, Vol. 1, 1981-1982, No. 23.

19. *John Paul II Speaks to Religious*, Vol. 5, 1987-1988, No. 152.

20. *LG*, 44.

Epilogue

1. *John Paul II Speaks to Religious*, Vol. 4, 1985-1986, No. 83.

QUESTIONS FOR
REFLECTION AND DISCUSSION

CHAPTER 1–The Divine Call

1. Read and reflect on the scriptural accounts of the calls and responses of the Old Testament figures referred to in this chapter. Use end notes for references.

2. What demands did Jesus make of those whom He invited to be His followers?

3. What is the significance of Jesus' encounter with the rich young man? (Mk 10:17-23)

4. The young man longed for "the more" but went away sad. What might have been the thoughts of Jesus as he walked away?

5. What might have been the far-reaching effects of the young man's rejection of the challenge Jesus put forth to him?

6. How could/does attachment to earthly things manifest itself in the daily living of those of us who are religious?

Supplementary Reading: *Redemptionis Donum*, nos. 1-3.

CHAPTER 2–The Call to Religious Profession

1. Discuss the commitment made by those professing the evangelical counsels and the commitment made by other Christians.

2. Reflect on the mysterious operation of the Trinity in your own call to the consecrated life. (See *Vita Consecrata*, nos. 15 and 16.)

   a. When did you first become aware of your call?

   b. How did your call develop?

   c. Were there difficulties involved?

   d. What prompted you to respond?

3. Chapter VI in *Lumen Gentium* is titled "Religious Life." Read sections 43 and 44 for further enrichment.

   a. Why, precisely, does a Christian make profession of the evangelical counsels in the Church?

   b. In what ways do the counsels bind the religious to the entire Church?

4. What does the Holy Father mean by "the person called experiences an *interior encounter* with the redeeming love of Christ?"

5. What are the demands of discipleship?

6. Why is prayer essential for living the life of the counsels?

7. What is the scriptural meaning of perfection?

8. How does a religious follow Christ radically?

9. How is the profession of the evangelical counsels a death/resurrection experience?

Supplementary Reading: *Redemptionis Donum,* nos. 4-6.

CHAPTER 3–Religious Consecration: A Sublime Mystery

1. Reflect on the meaning of "mission" as it is presented in this chapter.

2. How did the Son accomplish His mission?

3. What is the nature, purpose and development of the Church's mission in the world?

4. How do religious share in Christ's redemptive work?

5. In what sense is Christ the founder of religious life?

6. What is the role of the Holy Spirit in the "consecration" and "mission" of the Messiah?

    a. Reflect on the Father as the ultimate source of consecration.

    b. How did Christ live out His consecration?

7. In *Perfectae Caritatis* (no. 5) we read that religious profession "constitutes a special consecration which is deeply rooted in the baptismal consecration and is a fuller expression of it." Read *Redemptionis Donum* (no. 7) to see what the Pope has to say about this.

    a. How is religious profession a new burial in the death of Christ?

    b. In what sense is religious profession a "new" consecration?

    c. For further enrichment read sections 5-12 in *Essential Elements in the Church's Teachings on Religious Life,* May 31, 1983.

8. How is a consecrated person drawn into the mystery of *spousal union?*

9. Because of our consecration as religious, our love relationship to Christ is both spousal and redemptive. How do we deepen this intimacy with our divine Spouse?

Supplementary Reading: *Redemptionis Donum*, nos. 7, 8.

CHAPTER 4–The Evangelical Counsels: A Radical Following of Christ

1. What is meant by "the economy of the Redemption?"

    a. Why do the evangelical counsels have a "Christocentric characteristic?"

    b. What does this characteristic do for the religious?

2. Discuss the three sins typical of the "passing world."

a. How did they originate?

b. How do they affect human society?

c. How does religious consecration overcome the three-fold lust of the world?

3. What is meant by the "paschal dimension" of the evangelical counsels?

a. In what way is religious life like a martyrdom?

b. How are we drawn ever more deeply into the Paschal Mystery of Christ?

c. Discuss the effects of "paschal duality."

4. Can the vows ever be redefined? Give reasons for your answer.

5. Reflect on and discuss how the transformation of the world will be brought about.

Supplementary Reading: *Redemptionis Donum*, nos. 9,10.

Chapter 5–Consecrated Chastity

1. Reflect on the Trinitarian nature of the counsel of chastity.

2. Discuss the nuptial imagery in the Old Testament.

a. What does every marriage contract involve?

b. How did the Israelites come to "know" Yahweh?

3. How did Christ introduce a "new mode of living" in the New Testament?

a. When did believers first become aware of the mystery of virginity?

b. How did St. Paul help to deepen the meaning and under-standing of chastity?

4. How does the Holy Father explain Christ's statement regarding "eunuchs for the sake of the kingdom of heaven?"

5. Discuss the eschatological nature of chastity.

6. Reflect on the meaning of "spousal love."

    a. Discuss the role of the Holy Spirit in the daily living of our vow of chastity at deep levels.

    b. What must we constantly guard against?

7. What precisely is at the very heart of our religious identity?

8. Explain how our vow of chastity is significant for the Church.

Supplementary Reading: *Redemptionis Donum*, no. 11.

Chapter 6–Evangelical Poverty

1. History shows that the state of religious life is largely dependent upon the degree to which evangelical poverty is lived.

    a. Why are evangelical poverty and the quality of religious life interdependent?

    b. Do you see any "interdependence" between the general state of religious life today and the practice of evangelical poverty?

2. To what extent did Christ live poverty?

    a. How did His poverty enrich us?

    b. Why is evangelical poverty not just an addition to redemption?

3. God gave us a body with a built-in orientation toward things in the world.

    a. How did Adam and Eve relate to the world of things before the fall?

    b. What happened to human nature when they fell? (See *Catechism of the Catholic Church*, nos. 374-379; 402-406).

4. What is meant by the "redemptive mode?"

    a. How do we religious enter into this mode?

    b. How does the practice of evangelical poverty help the religious to grow in holiness?

5. What does "poor in spirit" mean for the religious?

     a. Reflect on and discuss the role of the Holy Spirit in our practice of poverty.

     b. What is essential for enriching others in a truly "redemptive" way?

6. How does the practice of evangelical poverty enrich others spiritually?

7. What does the Holy Father mean by the "salvific profile" of the poverty of Christ?

     a. Why is ongoing conversion of heart essential for entering into this profile?

     b. Why is the daily examen essential for spiritual growth?

8. How is evangelical poverty a witness?

Supplementary Reading: *Redemptionis Donum*, no. 12.

Chapter 7–Filial Obedience

1. The *Catechism of the Catholic Church* states that freedom is the power to act or not to act. It attains perfection in its acts when directed toward God, the sovereign Good (no. 1744).

     a. How does the counsel of obedience protect and promote our freedom?

     b. How does doing God's will bring us to fullness of life in Him? (See CCC, nos. 1730-1748).

2. Discuss the mystery of paschal duality (death/resurrection) in the obedience of Christ.

     a. How did Christ accomplish the Father's redemptive work?

     b. When did His obedience reach its climax?

     c. How did Christ's obedience win freedom for the human race? (See CCC, no. 1741).

     d. How is the counsel of obedience redemptive?

3. Reflect on the proper role of authority in community life.

a. What is the ecclesial dimension of religious authority?

b. How does a superior grow in likeness to Christ?

4. Explain how the vow of obedience is a continuation of Christ's own obedience to the Father.

5. How does our vow of obedience give us a share in the work of universal redemption?

6. Human authority is sometimes seen as a threat to one's freedom and independence.

a. How far-reaching might this distorted image of authority be directed?

b. Discuss ways in which human authority is sometimes undermined.

7. How do we religious live out the mystery of "paschal duality" in union with Christ?

8. How is Christian obedience related to filial obedience?

Supplementary Reading: *Redemptionis Donum*, no. 13.

CHAPTER 8–Religious Life in the Church

1. Read and reflect on no. 14 in *Redemptionis Donum*. Here we find the Holy Father expressing his interests and concerns of the Church regarding the consecrated life.

a. What are the hopes and expectations of the Church regarding religious life?

b. How can religious help to foster in the faithful a renewed ecclesial awareness?

c. How do religious "bear witness" to the redemption?

2. Read and reflect on no. 15 in *Redemptionis Donum*.

a. What is the specific mission of the consecrated person?

b. What is the truth at the basis of the whole economy of the redemption?

c. How do religious proclaim this truth?

3. Why is it important for religious to have a correct and complete understanding of the Church as the Council Fathers portrayed it in *Lumen Gentium*? (If you have not already read and reflected on *Lumen Gentium,* try to do so at your earliest opportunity. Give special attention to Chapter VI which is on Religious Life.)

4. Discuss/reflect upon how we religious are integrated into the Church and her mystery. On what is our apostolic fruitfulness dependent?

5. Why is it essential that the proper characteristics of religious life be in evidence at all times?

   a. Discuss/reflect upon these "characteristics."

   b. Why must our witness always be clear and consistent?

   c. What is it that prompts a joyful witness of our consecrated life at all times?

   d. Discuss/reflect upon the public witness value of religious life.

6. Discuss/reflect upon the Holy Father's teachings on the "apostolate."

   a. Where should our apostolate begin? What does this involve?

   b. Discuss/reflect upon: "What you do is important, but what you are is even more important."

Now read and discuss the final chapter in *Redemptionis Donum.*

SELECTED BIBLIOGRAPHY

Essential Elements in the Church's Teaching on Religious Life, Sacred Congregation for Religious and for Secular Institutes, Boston: Daughters of St. Paul, 1983.

Gambari, Elio, *Journey Toward Renewal,* Boston: Daughters of St. Paul, 1968.

Gambari, Elio, *Renewal of Religious Life,* Boston: Daughters of St. Paul, 1967.

John Paul II Speaks to Religious, Vols. 1-10, Baltimore: distributed by the Little Sisters of the Poor. (Principal allocutions and letters of John Paul II to religious from 1978-1998; compiled and arranged with a Synopsis by John Beyer, S.J.)

Redemptionis Donum, Boston: Daughters of St. Paul, 1984. (Apostolic Exhortation of His Holiness Pope John Paul II to men and women religious in the light of the Mystery of the Redemption.)

Sheets, John, S.J., Retreat on *Redemptionis Donum* given at Carmel of Danvers. (The content from this retreat presented in *An Undivided Heart* was drawn from audio tapes.)

Sheets, John, S.J., "The Primordial Mystery of Consecration," *Review for Religious*, Sept./Oct., 1985.

St. Teresa of Avila, *The Collected Works of St. Teresa of Avila,* Vol. One, trans. Kavanaugh, OCD, and Rodriguez, OCD, Washington D.C.: ICS Publications, 1987.

The Code of Canon Law, Grand Rapids: Eerdmans Pub., 1983. (English translation.)

The Holy Bible, San Francisco: Ignatius Press, 1966. (Revised Standard Version, Catholic Edition.)

Vatican Council II, New York: Costello Pub. Co., 1975. (Edited by Austin Flannery, O.P.)

Visible Signs of the Gospel: Messages of John Paul II on Consecrated Life, Boston: Daughters of St. Paul, 1980.

Vita Consecrata, Boston: Pauline Books and Media, 1996. (Post-Synodal Apostolic Exhortation of Pope John Paul II.)

Von Speyr, Adrienne, "Meditations on John," *The Farewell Discourses*, Vol. 3, San Francisco: Ignatius Press, 1987.

EXPLANATION OF THE COVER ICON

"Consecrated Life at the Service of the Church"
by the iconographer
Rev. Msgr. Anthony A. La Femina, S.T.L., J.C.D.

The icon featured on the cover celebrates its theme by presenting an allegory of the Church. The Church is a mysterious reality that cannot be totally expressed by a human concept because it is divine as well as human. Therefore, many allegories are necessary to describe the various aspects of the Church's reality.

The icon portrays a heavenly scene in the golden mandorla shown in the firmament. The Church is presented as "the sinless Bride of Christ, the joyful Mother of a great company of saints' (Preface 53). As Bride, she wears a golden wedding band shaped as a cross. She is clothed in garments of red and white to signify her supernatural character, and green to indicate her human side. Holy Mother Church possesses royal dignity because she, one with her Spouse, is to announce and establish the kingdom of God and His Messiah. Her crown is decorated with Host, chalice and crossed keys, symbolizing the Sacrament of Holy Orders. The Host and chalice symbolize the Eucharistic Action that made present the Sacrifice of Calvary at the Last Supper and continues to make it present until the end of time. The Church owes her origin to the Eucharistic Sacrifice of Holy Thursday and for this reason she is eucharistic by her very nature. Through this Sacrament Holy Mother Church has power in the Holy Spirit to offer her divine Lord's very own Sacrifice, together with herself, to the Heavenly Father and to transform sinners into saints by forgiving sin.

The Church has been entrusted with Seven Sacraments for her evangelizing task of sanctifying humanity. The clasp holding Holy

91

Mother Church's mantle contains seven diamonds. They represent the six Sacraments surrounding the most blessed Eucharist, which is simultaneously a Sacrifice-Sacrament, a Communion-Sacrament, and a Presence-Sacrament (*Redemptor hominis*, n. 81). All the other Sacraments are bound up with the Eucharist and oriented toward it since in it is contained Christ Himself. The Eucharist is thus the very center and apex of the life of all the Church's children; it is the living and superabundant Source of God's every grace.

In the icon Holy Mother Church humbly kneels in adoring contemplation before her divine Bridegroom. Rays of red and white light emanate from His sacred breast, depicting Divine Mercy according to the revelations to St. Faustina Kowalska of the Most Blessed Sacrament, the first canonized saint of the present millennium. The red light signifies the Lord's Precious Blood, which is the life of souls, and recalls the Eucharist, which makes present the Sacrifice of Calvary. The white light denotes the Water from the crucified Lord's heart. It brings to mind the Gift of the Holy Spirit, who makes souls holy and pleasing to God through the remission of sin in the Sacraments of Baptism and Reconciliation. The Lord Jesus stated in His first messianic declaration that His mission consists in revealing God's mercy to humanity, which is needy, oppressed, blind and captive (Lk 4:18,19). It is therefore imperative that Holy Mother Church keep in mind the Father's mercy, which is incarnated and personified in her beloved Spouse. She must constantly bear witness to God's mercy and implore it in the face of all the manifestations of physical and moral evil, before all the threats that cloud the whole horizon of the life of humanity (*Dives in misericordia*, n. 125). Mother Church must proclaim to humanity that love must condition justice so that justice may serve love. Love is transformed into mercy when it is necessary to go beyond the norm of justice. The relationship between justice and love is manifested precisely in mercy. Mercy is what God is, and what he desires (Mt 9:13; Hos. 6:6); and God's mercy is what consecrated persons must bring to mankind in their service of evangelization on behalf of the Church. In the Eucharist they find both the Source and School of that mercy which God desires for and from all humanity.

In the icon Holy Mother Church offers the matchless fruit of the True Vine that her consecrated sons and daughters on earth provide her, with for the glory of God the Father, by their service on behalf of the Church through their evangelizing work for the kingdom of God. The Lord Jesus says to Holy Mother Church: "My Father has been glorified in your bearing much fruit and becoming my disciples" (Jn 15:8). These words are applicable in a particular way to consecrated persons since they have voluntarily accepted the Lord's invitation to seek evangelical perfection, which requires that they hand over their lives to Him in a completely selfless manner for service to the kingdom.

The incomparable fruit that consecrated persons bear for the glory of the Father is the fruit of the True Vine, who is Jesus Messiah, the Son of God. He alone can produce this inimitable fruit because he is who he is (Ex 3:14), and the branches can do nothing apart from the Vine (Jn 15:5,6). Consecrated persons are able to bear this fruit only through their personal union with the Lord Jesus and by the strength that God Himself provides for them (1 Pt 4:11). Not even one's own native talents come from oneself. God provides every one of His gifts with a view to man's salvation. Hence the significance of St. Paul's humbling words: "This is not your own doing, it is God's gift; neither is it a reward for anything you have accomplished, so let no one pride himself on it. We are truly His handiwork, created in Christ Jesus to lead the life of good deeds which God prepared for us in advance" (Eph 2:8-10).

Consecrated persons bearing fruit at the service of Holy Mother Church are pictured in the icon in the globe symbolizing earth. As they receive Divine Mercy from on high, so must they bestow this mercy through their evangelizing service. The earth is suspended in the firmament and around it are the four seraphic figures of the evangelists that come forth from the throne of God (Ezk 1:10; Rev 4:7). Only those upon earth need evangelization; and consecrated men and women, whether in active or contemplative life, carry out this service that implements the Lord Jesus' New Covenant commandment: "love one another as I have loved you" (Jn 13:34,35). Evangelization is a many faceted work that is realized through the performance of the corporal and spiritual works of mercy. These works are the practical translations of the Church's proposals of life and her message of love. They are so important that the Lord made them the divine norm for His final judgment of mankind. But clearly, the greater obligation for their performance rests upon His consecrated men and women. Through their works of mercy at the service of His Church, the Lord Jesus desires to continue His work of revealing to all mankind His loving Father (Jn 17:26), who is the "Father of mercies" (2 Cor 1:3). Only by dedicated evangelization can the world come to know both Jesus, whom the Father commands it to hear, and to know the Heavenly Father, whose perfection it must imitate.

All consecrated men and women must perform the sacred duty of evangelization by reason of the special profession of their particular state of life. They are portrayed in the icon with golden shoes, reflecting the words of Isaiah: "How beautiful upon the mountains are the feet of him who brings glad tidings" (Is 52:7; Rom 10:15). "To evangelize" means "to bring glad tidings." Unfortunately, however, the terrain of evangelization is mountainous and craggy; and the message of evangelization often encounters physical and moral violence. However, it depends in great part upon consecrated persons, by reason of their voluntarily professed service to Holy Mother Church, to transform the hostile world by an evangelization centered upon the Eucharist so that the world may become hospitable to the civilization of love in which the God who is love (1 Jn 4:8,16) may reign sovereign. Undaunted fortitude and serene perseverance are needed, but the Lord – the Martyr of evangelization - promises His very own accompanying presence to those who follow Him through service to His Church in His all-embracing work of eucharistic evangelization for the glory of the Father: "Do not be distressed or fearful…. the Prince of this world is at hand. He has no hold on me…. Come, then! Let us be on our way" (Jn 15:27,30,31).

Anyone interested in purchasing a print of Msgr. La Femina's icon should write the INSTITUTE ON RELIGIOUS LIFE, P.O. Box 41007, Chicago, IL 60641 or call 773-267-1195.